THE INSIDE TRACK LIBRARY

The
Stock Market

INSIDE TRACK

THE INSIDE TRACK LIBRARY

The Stock Market

Nancy Dunnan

SILVER BURDETT PRESS

Published by Silver Burdett Press, Inc., a division of Simon & Schuster, Inc., Prentice Hall
Bldg., Englewood Cliffs, NJ 07632.

Created and produced by: Blackbirch Graphics, Inc.

Project Editor: Emily Easton
Designer: Cynthia Minichino

Manufactured in the United States of America

10 9 8 7 6 5 4 3 2 1

Library of Congress Cataloging-in-Publication Data

Dunnan, Nancy.
  The stock market / Nancy Dunnan.
  (Inside track)
  Includes bibliographical references.
  Summary: Describes what stocks are, how they are bought and
sold, and the functions and operation of stock exchanges.
    1. Stock-exchanges—United States—Juvenile literature.
2. Stocks-United States—Juvenile literature.   [1. Stock exchange.
2. Stocks.]   I. Title. II. Series.
HG4910.D84   1990   332.64′273—dc20
ISBN 0-382-09914-1 (lib. bdg.)   90-31175
ISBN 0-382-24025-1 (pbk.)   CIP
                                         AC

(Frontispiece)
A frenetic day on the Tokyo Stock Exchange.

CONTENTS

The Cathedrals of Wall Street (1944), a homage to American capitalism by Florine Stettheimer.

WHAT IS A STOCK?

Question: What do an IBM PC, a pair of Reebok sneakers and a Ford Mustang have in common? *Answer:* *The three corporations that manufacture these products trade their stocks on the New York Stock Exchange.*

That means you can buy a pair of Reebok jogging shoes as well as a part of the company that makes them. You can find the shoes at a store near your home, but to own a part of the company you must buy its **stock** from a stockbroker. A stock represents part ownership in a company. Anyone who owns stock is called a **stockholder** or a **shareholder.** Reebok International is actually owned by its stockholders—thousands of men, women, and institutions—each one with part ownership in the company. If Reebok International makes a profit selling shoes to the

Stock: *An ownership share in a company. Companies sell stock to raise money. People buy stock as an investment, anticipating that it will rise in price.*

Stockholder: *An individual or organization who owns stock in a company; also known as a shareholder.*

public, you will too, because your stock in the company will rise in value. But, of course, if Reebok shoes fade in popularity and Americans favor New Balance or L.A. Gear instead, then the price of your Reebok stock will drop. This movement up and down in price is what makes owning stock such an exciting process. You can participate in the action.

How a Company Is Organized: The Reebok Story

Every business day, millions of shares of stock are bought and sold in this country. Where does the money come from? Let's look at one company, Reebok, to find the answer.

Reebok shoes made their first appearance in the 1890s when Joseph William Foster of Bolton, England, fashioned for himself a pair of track shoes with spikes in them. These special shoes became so popular with Foster's friends and neighbors that by 1895 he went into business making them by hand for other runners. During World Wars I and II, J.W. Foster and Sons was known for its army boots. By the 1950s it had expanded into rugby and soccer shoes.

Then, in 1958, two of the founder's grandsons, Joseph and Jeffrey Foster, started a companion firm called Reebok. Reebok eventually absorbed J.W. Foster and Sons.

Reebok shoes were virtually unknown in the United States until 1979, when an American marketer of outdoor equipment, Paul Fireman, spotted Reebok shoes at an international sporting goods exhibition. He was so impressed by their quality that he decided to market Reeboks in the United States.

In 1985, Fireman and others decided to merge the American and British firms and form one corporation called Reebok International, Ltd. Businesses can be set up in a number of different ways with each having different advantages and disadvantages. Fireman and his associates chose the corporate structure because this legal form protects them and any other investors from financial claims that might be made. If, for example, the business failed, as is the case with many new operations, then the company's **creditors** usually have the right to take the company's **assets** as payment for its debt. In a corporation, the financial risks for the owners and investors are limited to the amount of money that they have invested, and no more. If Reebok failed as a company and owed millions of dollars, its investors would not personally be responsible for that debt.

The newly merged company of Reebok International then formed a **board of directors**, a group responsible for overseeing the company's affairs. In 1985, the Reebok board of directors voted to **go public**, that is, to sell shares of stock to the public in order to raise money for company expansion.

How Stocks Are Issued

When a company wants to raise **capital** to expand, it can borrow the money from a bank or it can issue, or sell, stocks to the public. Reebok decided to sell stocks. Stocks are sold to the public in two steps, initially in the primary market. Thereafter these same stocks are resold to other investors in the secondary market.

An **investment banker,** who is usually employed by a large investment firm, is hired by companies such as Reebok to help with this process. The investment banker, along with his firm's

Creditor: One to whom money is owed.

Assets: Anything a person, company, or group owns or is owed, such as money, investments, property, inventory, and equipment.

Board of directors: A group of people elected by a company's stockholders, who are responsible for setting the company's basic policy.

Go public: When a company sells its own shares to the public to raise money.

Capital: The money needed to start or expand a business.

Investment banker: The middleman between a corporation issuing new stocks and the public. The investment banker arranges the company's financing by buying a new issue of stocks and selling them to individuals and institutions.

Securities and Exchange Commission (SEC): A federal agency created in 1934 to regulate the investment industry and protect the public. It is headed up by five commissioners appointed on a rotating basis by the President of the United States.

Portfolio: A holding or ownership of more than one stock, bond, commodity or other asset by an individual or institutional investor. A diversified portfolio reduces risk.

analysts, studies the company and the market and determines a fair price for the stock. The investment banking firm then buys all the stock from the company for resale to the public at the best possible price. This is called underwriting.

If a large number of shares are being issued, the investment banker may bring in others to share in the cost of purchase. This is called a syndicate. The shares are sold to the public by everyone in the syndicate at a fixed price.

Before the first stock could be sold, Reebok had to file a registration statement with the **Securities and Exchange Commission (SEC)**. The Reebok

A typical stock certificate.

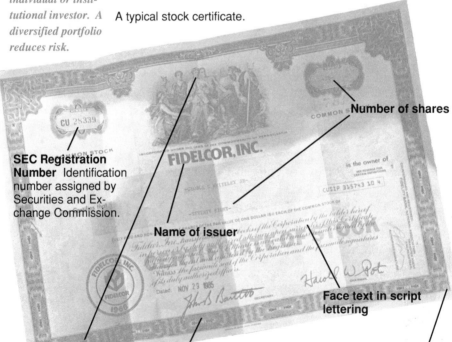

Number of shares

SEC Registration Number Identification number assigned by Securities and Exchange Commission.

Name of issuer

Face text in script lettering

Human figures This extremely detailed artwork makes the certificate difficult to counterfeit. All NYSE certificates must show at least a 3/4 view of a human being.

Geometric lathe work At least 20 square inches of this detail must be displayed. These patterns can only be duplicated if the exact machine settings are known.

Planchettes These are the small, chemically treated, colored disks in the stock certificate paper. The chemicals further identify the certificate as authentic.

YOUR FINANCIAL NOTEBOOK

Now that you are beginning to learn about the stock market, you can set up your own financial notebook. A loose-leaf type with rings is best because you can update and discard pages as you gather information. Divide your notebook into categories of interest, such as:

- *New words.* Keep an ongoing list of unfamiliar words; look up their definitions in this book or in a financial dictionary.
- *Companies.* Write down the names of local companies that you are interested in, and their phone numbers. Find out if you can buy their stock. Staple or tape articles about the company into the notebook.
- *Stockbrokers.* Keep a list of brokerage firms or names of stockbrokers you read or hear about.
- *Stocks.* Write down any stocks you buy (or are interested in buying) and track their prices and dividend payouts.
- *Radio and television programs.* Note the times and stations of your favorite financial broadcasts. Jot down specific stock recommendations given by experts. Develop a sample **portfolio** and track its performance.
- *Miscellaneous.* Note anything else related to Wall Street and the stock market that you feel might be useful in the future.

registration statement contained hundreds of details about the company's financial condition and its overall business. Many of these facts and figures were also printed in a **prospectus**, a document given to all potential investors in Reebok stock. This entire process of going public, in which part of a company is sold to outside investors, is called an initial public offering, or IPO.

The initial public offering is the only time the price of a stock is fixed. After its first sale, it fluctuates, depending upon supply and demand.

When a company goes public it must of course let the investment world know. It does this by

Prospectus: The official public report that a company must give to prospective buyers of its newly issued stock. It provides financial details, the firm's history, a list of officers, and a description of any pending legal problems—all information to help investors decide whether or not to purchase the stock.

placing ads in the financial press, such as *The Wall Street Journal, The New York Times*, and *Barron's*. These ads are called tombstones. Why? Some say that with their black borders and heavy dark ink, they resemble graveyard tombstones. Others maintain that the way the names are arranged is similar to the format on gravestones. Tombstones give important facts about the company to potential investors.

Common and Preferred Stock

Everyone who purchased a share of Reebok stock, either back in 1985 when it went public or today, is called a shareholder, or part owner of the company. How much each person owns is determined by the number of shares that were purchased. Today there are 113 million Reebok shares, so owning one would mean owning 1/113 millionth of the company. But no matter how large or small your ownership is, you own a part of every building, piece of machinery or equipment, and whatever else the company owns.

In order to document the fact that people purchase shares in Reebok, the company issues a **stock certificate** to each shareholder. This piece of paper shows the number of shares owned by that person.

Companies can issue two types of stock: common and preferred. If the company is profitable, the owners of common stock share in the profits in two ways: one, they gain income through **dividends** and dividend increases; and two, they benefit as the stock increases in price, known as **capital appreciation**.

After common stock is issued, a corporation may decide to issue preferred stock. Dividends are paid to preferred stockholders before being distrib-

Stock certificate: A piece of paper or computerized entry showing ownership of a stock. A certificate includes the issuer's name (i.e., the corporation), the number of shares and the name of the owner of the stock. The back contains details for transferring ownership.

Dividend: A periodic payment from a company's earnings to stockholders. Most dividends are paid four times a year. Dividends can increase, decrease, or be cancelled, depending upon the company's profits.

Capital appreciation: Also known as capital gain. Profit made on stocks when sold at a higher price than they originally cost.

Liquidate: When a company fails, its assets are converted back into cash and this money is used to pay off debts.

WAYS COMPANIES CAN RAISE MONEY

When a company wants to expand, devote more effort to research, or buy property or equipment, it must raise money. It can do this by selling **securities** to the public or by borrowing money. The term securities refers to an investment that shows ownership in a company, such as a stock or a creditor relationship such as a a bond. And, there are other ways to obtain cash.

- *Form a partnership.* An owner can merge with another person who is willing to invest money.
- *Reinvest profits.* After paying its annual expenses, a company can pour the leftover money back into the business. This money is called retained earnings.
- *Borrow.* Bank loans are an immediate source of capital, but the loan eventually must be paid back plus a fee for borrowing, known as **interest.** Interest is a yearly fee, figured as a percentage of the loan. For example, if a company borrows $1 million at a 9 percent interest rate, the annual interest payments are $90,000.
- *Issue bonds.* Bonds are issued by companies to the public. The bond is actually an I.O.U., indicating that the company has borrowed a set amount of money. After a specified time the bond matures, or "comes due," and the company must pay back the loan amount to the investor. During the time the company had use of the loan money, it must pay regular interest to the investor or bondholder.
- *Sell stocks.* By selling shares of stock, or part ownership in the company to the public, companies can raise large amounts of money. They do not have to pay interest on this but they do have to give up some control over the company's operations in return for the investor's money.

uted to common stockholders. And, if the company runs into serious trouble and is forced to **liquidate**, preferred shareholders will receive their investment back before the common shareholders receive theirs. Preferred stocks usually cost more than common stocks. In return for this preferential treatment, however, preferred shareholders only get

Interest: The cost of borrowing money stated as a yearly fee, and figured as a percentage of the loan.

a fixed dividend. Even if the board of directors votes to increase the dividend on common stock, the dividend on the preferred stock will remain the same.

Voting Rights

Stockholders are entitled to vote on certain issues, such as who should be on the board of directors. In the case of Reebok, each share is equal to one vote, so a shareholder with ten shares can cast ten votes. The board appoints the top management and decides whether more stock should be issued, and whether dividends should be paid. It determines broad corporate policy but does not run the company on a day-to-day basis. For that, it elects a president and other officers.

Quarter: A three-month period, representing 1/4, or 25 percent, of the year.

Most boards meet once a **quarter** to listen to management's reports on the company's financial status and its plans for the future.

Annual meeting: The once-a-year gathering of a corporation's directors, officers, and shareholders at which time new directors are elected, the results of the past year are discussed, and shareholder resolutions are voted on.

Once a year, Reebok also holds an **annual meeting** in Boston that all stockholders can attend. At this gathering, management makes its annual report to shareholders. The SEC requires that all publicly traded companies distribute the annual report to shareholders. The annual report is a yearly record of a corporation's growth, as well as a financial report card describing sales, earnings, losses, and the financial results for the year just ended. (In Chapter 6 you will learn how to read an annual report.) At the annual meeting, any stockholder, even someone who owns just one share, can make suggestions or ask questions.

Proxy: Written authority to act for another person. Proxies are sent to shareholders by corporate management in order to obtain their authority to vote the shareholders' shares at the annual meeting.

At an annual meeting, stockholders are sometimes required to vote on certain matters. If a stockholder cannot attend and vote in person, he or she signs an absentee ballot, called a **proxy**. This

A sample proxy card.

paper is mailed to all shareholders before the meeting and has yes or no boxes to be checked off for each proposal. Or, the stockholder can authorize his or her votes to be cast along with those of the board of directors. Sometimes there is a proxy fight in which each side tries to get as many signed proxies as possible to support its position.

Where Do the Profits Go?

But let's return to Reebok. As the company grew in size and made more money, the board voted to share some of these profits with the shareholders in the form of a dividend. Dividend amounts vary from stock to stock. In fact, some companies never pay dividends. Those that consistently pay dividends are known as **income stocks**, and investors buy them precisely because they want the steady

Income stock: A stock with a high-dividend yield, such as electric utility stocks.

cash payments. Some corporations reinvest most of their profits in the business in order to help it expand. The stock of companies that pay little or no dividends are known as **growth stocks**. Investors buy them because they expect the company and the price of the stock to grow.

Reebok currently pays its stockholders a dividend of 30 cents per share. It is paid over the year in quarterly payments of 7.5 cents each. This means stockholders receive four dividend checks per year. An equal dividend is paid for each share of stock, so the more shares you own, the larger your dividend check will be. A shareholder with 100 shares will earn $30.00 in dividends each year.

Reebok does not share all its yearly profits with stockholders because the company needs most of this money to expand its business. This money is called retained earnings.

By using its own earnings to finance expansion and growth, the company reduces the amount it needs to borrow from a bank. This particular type of financing is called internal financing because the money comes from inside the company and not from outside sources. When a company borrows from external sources, such as a bank, it must pay interest on the loan. It is less expensive for the company to use internal financing than to borrow money.

Stock Splits

Dividends are not the only way of rewarding stockholders. Sometimes the company's directors do not want to pay out a cash dividend, so they declare a **stock split** as a way of benefiting stockholders. Another reason for stock splits is to reduce the price of a company's stock so that more people will buy it.

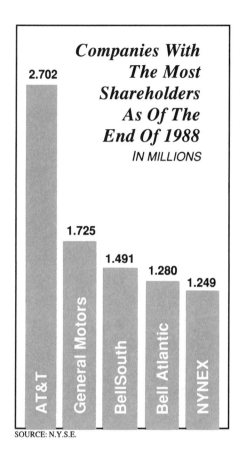

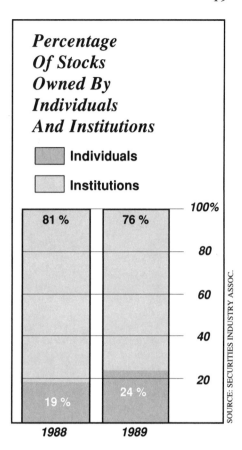

In 1986 Reebok management felt its stock was
so high in price that it was discouraging new investors from buying it. The board of directors, therefore, decided to split the shares three for one. Stock
splits can also be two for one, ten for one, or any
other combination. Reebok split its stock again in
1987. This time it was a two for one split.

A stock split does not immediately change the
value of each person's holdings. A stock worth $60
that is split two for one results in two shares, each
worth $30.

Stocks for Sale
You may buy stock in any publicly held corporation—one whose shares are traded publicly. Unlike

Reebok, many American companies are privately held. These companies are owned by a handful of people, often family and a few others, who hold most of the shares and control the company. Reebok was privately held until 1985 when it went through its initial public offering.

In addition to public shareholders such as you and me, institutions also buy shares in corporations. Institutional investors include employee pension funds and **mutual funds**, such as Fidelity Investments Co., that have huge sums to invest for members of their organization. If the institution is large enough, it can affect the price of a stock because it buys and sells so many shares.

Mutual fund: An investment corporation that sells shares to the public. Investors' money is used to buy shares of stocks and other securities. The fund is run by a professional portfolio manager who decides what to buy and sell.

The Secondary Market

Once a company's first, or initial, public offering of stock is sold, its shares then trade in the secondary market. The secondary market is not any one place but includes the New York and American exchanges plus a handful of **regional stock exchanges** as well as the **over-the-counter market.** A stock exchange is a market place where **listed** stocks, those that have been approved by the exchange for trading, are bought and sold. The exchanges do not own the stocks, nor do they influence the prices. The exchange functions as an auction for stocks. Prices are determined by buyers and sellers.

Regional exchanges : An exchange that specializes in stocks of that region, rather than those with national interest. Regional exchanges also trade many of the securities traded on the NYSE and AMEX.

A stock's price at any given time depends on what people are willing to pay for it. Current events, such as presidential elections, war, and changes in interest rates, also affect stock prices.

The most famous exchange, and the one where Reebok stocks are bought and sold, is the New York Stock Exchange (NYSE). In the next chapter you will learn how the exchanges came into being.

Over-the-counter market : A nationwide network of stock-brokers who trade stocks not listed on an exchange.

Listed: A stock that is traded on one of the exchanges.

THE DARK SIDE OF WALL STREET: IVAN BOESKY

The one-time Wall Street superstar of the 1980s, Ivan Boesky, was sentenced in 1987 to three years in prison for his role in the largest insider trading scandal in history. The SEC defines insider trading as the illegal profiting from information about private corporate takeovers before that knowledge has been announced publicly. Boesky agreed to pay $100 million in penalties for his insider trading activities and he was barred for life from further trading in the United States.

Boesky, a shadowy figure whom very few people had ever heard of before the SEC investigation, was actually one of America's richest and most clever stock speculators. His specialty was called risk arbitrage—buying and selling stocks in companies that appear ready to be taken over by another company. Over the course of ten years, Boesky made an estimated $200 million through risk arbitrage.

Arbitrage based on public information is not illegal, but the use of secret tips or insider information, as Boesky sometimes did, is against SEC rules. In Boesky's case, the SEC charged he had contracted for insider information from David Levine, a takeover specialist with Drexel, Burnham, Lambert, an investment banking firm. Levine had advance data about takeover bids being made by one company for another.

Boesky apparently promised to give Levine a percentage of profits for his tips plus a $2.4 million lump-sum payment. Among the stocks the SEC cited in which Boesky profited illegally were Nabisco Brands, Houston Natural Gas, General Foods, Union Carbide, and Boise Cascade.

Boesky, who grew up in Detroit, Michigan, where his father operated a series of popular delicatessens, had been an accountant with no particular career direction until he hit Wall Street in 1966 and learned about risk arbitrage. He eventually set up his own firm, investing other people's money. During law school, he married the daughter of a wealthy real estate tycoon who apparently set him up in business. Some say Boesky was driven to become richer than his father-in-law. Whether this was true or not, he certainly was motivated by money. With an army of 100 employees, Boesky ran his operation from a plush Fifth Avenue office where he worked frantic 20 hour days. He often personally stood behind the firm's 300-line telephone console, pushing buttons, talking to clients and traders, and drinking gallons of black coffee, seemingly all at once. Boesky was forced to stop pushing buttons when the SEC stepped in and began unraveling what turned out to be Wall Street's very own Watergate.

Posting the notice that delineated Wall Street,1644. All citizens of the Dutch colony were ordered to report with "tools in hand" to aid in the construction of the wall.

HOW THE STOCK MARKET STARTED

Four hundred years ago, Wall Street was merely a dusty cow path at the lower tip of Manhattan. Today, however, it is the financial center of the world, with the most famous investment institution, the New York Stock Exchange (NYSE), located at 11 Wall Street. This and other stock exchanges provide meeting places for buyers and sellers to "exchange," or trade, stocks.

The term Wall Street also refers to the general financial community where stocks, bonds, **commodities**, and other investments are sold to the public. In this context, the phrase Wall Street includes the New York Stock Exchange, the American Stock Exchange (AMEX), the various regional exchanges, and the over-the-counter-market.

Commodities : Bulk goods, such as gold, silver, platinum, corn, wheat, cotton, rice, coffee, sugar, and cocoa.

In 1792, under a buttonwood tree, the stock exchange was started.

Early Trading: Furs, Molasses, and Tobacco

The name Wall Street comes from the wall or stockade built along the original path by the early Dutch settlers to protect themselves from Indians, pirates, and other dangers. The Dutch had established a trading post on the island of Manhattan shortly after Henry Hudson explored the area in 1609. In 1626 Peter Minuit, the head of the colony, made one of the greatest real-estate coups of all time and purchased the entire 22-square-mile island from the Indians for the sum of $24. The Dutch named their trading post New Amsterdam.

The path quickly became a bustling commercial street because it joined the docks on the East River with those to the west on the Hudson River. The early merchants built their warehouses and other businesses on this path, along with a city hall and a church. They primarily traded commodities: furs, molasses, tobacco, and wheat, as well as foreign currencies. Slaves were also bought and sold until the 1780s. Land speculation was popular, but stocks and bonds did not officially become part of Wall Street until after the Revolutionary War.

In 1664 the English took control of the settlement and renamed the tiny but growing area New York. After the Revolutionary War, New York was the capital of the United States from 1785 until 1790. Our first president, George Washington, was inaugurated on the steps of what is now Federal Hall on Wall Street. Today, on the approximate spot where Washington took the oath, there is a statue of him by the New York sculptor J.Q.A. Ward. The sculptures in the pediments of the New York Stock Exchange are also by Ward.

Revolutionary War Bonds

In the beginning only commodities were traded; there were no stocks or bonds as we know them.

Things began to change, however, when the federal government was established. Alexander Hamilton, the great financial thinker, was chosen secretary of the treasury. In January 1790, he suggested that the new government pay off the debt that the thirteen states had accumulated during the Revolutionary War by issuing bonds.

One of the initial acts of the first Congress when it met at Federal Hall was to authorize the sale of 6 percent government war bonds to pay off the $80 million war debt. Brokers, congressmen, and others went wild, trying to make their fortune in these bonds, the first national securities sold to the public.

The First Stock

A few years later, bank stocks were sold to the public. Again it was Hamilton's idea. He established the First Bank of the United States and sold shares to the public at $100. Other bank and insurance company stocks were soon added to the list of available securities.

Hamilton, who put the process of selling securities in motion, did not live to see the formation of the New York Stock Exchange. Thirteen years before the exchange's charter was drawn up, Vice-President Aaron Burr shot Secretary of the Treasury Hamilton in a duel on July 11, 1804. Hamilton died the next day. Hamilton and Burr had been political enemies for years. Hamilton had used his considerable power to prevent Burr from becoming President. Burr accused Hamilton of calling him a "dangerous man" and challenged him to a duel. Hamilton deliberately misfired before Burr fired with the intent to kill.

Hamilton is buried in Trinity Churchyard, at the head of his beloved Wall Street, where he had lived and worked most of his life.

At first, news about stocks reached people informally—primarily through discussions in coffeehouses and ads in newspapers. The early dealers were not stockbrokers as much as they were auctioneers and merchants. Merchants sold some of these securities over the counter in their shops, just as they sold buttons, fabric, grain, and other supplies. Securities were also sold outdoors on the street and at auctions. Independent auctioneers ran public stock auctions at the east end of Wall Street. Investors used brokers to attend the auctions and buy and sell for them. Not surprisingly, the brokers and auctioneers became rivals, each wanting to gain control of the growing market.

The brokers eventually went their own way, meeting under a large buttonwood tree on Wall Street.

Without a formal and centralized trading place, and with the auctioneers and brokers at opposite ends of Wall Street, investing was not a simple task at that time. Unethical practices were common and chaos reigned more often than not.

Under the Buttonwood Tree

In March 1792 twenty-four of New York's leading merchants met secretly at Corre's Hotel to discuss ways to bring order to the securities business and to wrest it from their competitors, the auctioneers. Two months later, on May 17, 1792, these men signed a document called the Buttonwood Agreement, named after their traditional meeting place. It stated that they would only trade securities among themselves, that they would adhere to set **commissions**, and not participate in other auctions. These twenty-four men were the founders of today's New York Stock Exchange.

Commission : The fee paid to a stockbroker for making a trade. The fee amount is determined by the number of shares traded and their price.

"We the Subscribers, Brokers for the Purchase and Sale of Public Stock, do hereby solemnly promise and pledge ourselves to each other, that we will not buy or sell from this day for any person whatsoever, any kind of Public Stock, at less than one quarter of one percent Commission on the Specie value and that we will give preference to each other in our Negotiations. In Testimony whereof we have set our hands this 17th day of May at New York, 1792."

The signers continued to meet regularly under their tree, and soon they began to take business away from the auctioneers.

By 1793 there were too many brokers involved to meet under a tree. So they took space in an elaborate structure on the corner of Wall and Water

Streets called the Tontine Coffee House. The Tontine, a merchant's exchange, was built by more than two hundred businessmen, known as subscribers, who paid $200 each for their ownership share. The brokers met in a room under the eaves; apparently it was hot, because on sunny days they continued to meet outside.

After the wild speculative fever over war bonds and stock in the Bank of the United States died down, trading on Wall Street was slow. Newspapers paid little attention to the securities business, although on March 10, 1815, the *New York Commercial Advertiser* carried a "complete list" of twenty-four stocks. Most were government securities and bank stocks. There was only one manufacturing company.

Opening of the New York Stock Exchange

The Buttonwood Agreement came too late for New York to have the nation's first stock exchange. That honor goes to Philadelphia, which opened an exchange in 1790. In fact, realizing it was losing business to that city, New York sent an observer to Philadelphia in early 1817. He returned bursting with the news of the thriving exchange. The New York Stock and Exchange Board was formally organized on March 8, 1817.

The first president of the exchange was Anthony Stockholm. The exchange rented a room at 40 Wall Street for $200 a year, including janitor services. Every morning when the exchange opened, the president read the stocks to be traded. After each stock was announced, the members shouted out bids and offers from their assigned seats. This was the origin of the phrase "to own a seat" on the exchange. The business day started about 11:30 A.M. and was usually finished by 1 P.M. Continuous daylong trading did not come into practice until years later. Contracts were paid for by 2:15 P.M. the following day, a practice that was in effect for more than one hundred years.

From the first, the exchange was an exclusive organization. New members needed to be voted in, and just three votes against an applicant meant he wasn't accepted! In 1817 a seat cost only $25. By 1827 the price of membership was $100. In 1848 it had reached $400.

Members wore top hats and swallowtail coats. Troublesome members were quickly brought in line with a series of fines: $5 for smoking a cigar, $10 for standing on a seat, $10 for throwing a paper dart, and 50 cents for knocking off a member's hat. Fines were also imposed for interrupting a call or using unacceptable language.

Business hit bottom on March 16, 1830, when only two stocks traded, with a total value of $3,470. Interest in stocks grew, however, as the country grew. The Mohawk and Hudson Railroad, the first railroad stock listed, started trading in 1830. Soon millions of dollars in securities were issued for building canals, roads, and railroads.

As trading volume increased, the NYSE expanded its hours and eventually gave up the call system. It was simply too noisy and too cumbersome to take verbal bids on so many stocks. In its place, the exchange allowed continuous trading throughout the day. No sale could be for less than five shares, with ten shares the standard size order.

The Noisy Curbstone Brokers

The only other exchange that rivaled the New York Stock Exchange was the Curb Exchange. Although

An early nineteenth century view of the Curb Market from Trinity Church.

it had existed informally for years, it grew in size and importance during the gold rush era, when mining and railroad stocks became extremely popular. Members of the established New York Stock Exchange regarded many of these issues as too risky, leaving a void that nonmember brokers quickly filled. Most of these brokers could not afford offices, so they conducted their business on the street. By the 1870s the corner of William and Beaver Streets was filled with brokers doing business outside, rain or shine. The corner was known as the Curb and the brokers were called curbstone brokers.

In the early 1890s the Curb moved to Broad Street. As its name indicates, Broad Street was much wider and provided more space for brokers. Many brokers also rented offices in the Mills Building. Inside, telephone clerks took orders and then stood on the wide window ledges or hung precariously out the windows, shouting orders down to the stockbrokers standing in the street. With everyone yelling at once the noise was unbearable, so the clerks developed a system of hand signals. To make it easy for the clerks to find them in the crowd, the brokers wore colored jackets and stood by the same lamppost each day.

Emanual S. Mendels, Jr., a curbstone broker with inclinations toward orderliness, tried to organize the Curb in 1908 by setting up the Curb Market Agency. The brokers were too wild to harness, though, and the agency was unable to enforce its own rules. In 1911 Mendels and others drew up a formal constitution and established the New York Curb Market Association. This time, Mendels was successful, and success brought an end to the Curb's free-wheeling outdoor business. On June 27, 1921, the Curb's chairman, Edward McCormick, led the rowdy brokers in a march up Wall Street to their new building on Trinity Place behind Trinity Church. As they marched, they sang "The Star-Spangled Banner" at the top of their lungs. But the curbstone brokers refused to forget their more carefree days. Inside the new quarters, each trading post was marked by a lamppost, a reminder of their more boisterous days outside.

In 1929 the Curb changed its name to the New York Curb Exchange and finally, in 1953, to the American Stock Exchange.

An early trading post on the floor of the exchange about 1910.

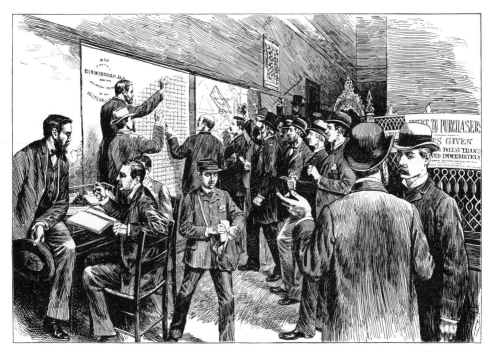

A nineteenth century engraving of the Birmingham, Alabama, Stock Exchange.

Today the Curb and the Buttonwood Tree are but memories and members of the exchange have no time to sit. Yet the New York and American Stock exchanges are both still private associations where members must buy their "seats." But membership, like the cost of land on the island of Manhattan, is considerably more expensive than when the Buttonwood traders struck their deals! Today a seat costs $550,000 on the New York Stock Exchange, $180,000 on the American.

ALEXANDER HAMILTON

Alexander Hamilton, who was the country's first Secretary of the Treasury, set out to restore the young country's wavering credit. He was born in the West Indies and sailed to the American colonies as a young man. While still a student, he wrote pamphlets supporting the colonial cause and served in the Revolutionary War, where his brilliance quickly attracted George Washington's attention. He soon became Washington's aide-de-camp and secretary.

After the war, Hamilton became a wealthy lawyer and prominent New Yorker, especially following his marriage to Elizabeth Schuyler, a member of a powerful New York family. His social and business connections helped tie the new government to men of wealth and position. However, his politics alienated the rural population and others who feared a strong central government.

Eventually, two opposing parties were formed: the Federalists, led by Hamilton and John Adams, and the Democratic Republicans, led by Thomas Jefferson and James Madison.

As Secretary of the Treasury under President Washington, Hamilton proposed that the debt accumulated by the Continental Congress be paid in full. The American colonies had borrowed $80 million to finance the Revolutionary War, but by 1781, the continental currency had collapsed. Hamilton proposed redeeming the continental currency at face value in bonds in order to instill confidence in the new government. Jefferson argued against this move because he felt it would only benefit the wealthy and drain the government's funds. However, he compromised and Hamilton's bill passed Congress.

Hamilton also chartered the Bank of New York and tried to keep competing banks from starting. But here he ran up against Aaron Burr, another lawyer who felt that concentration of power was dangerous, and wanted the bulk of power to be controlled by the individual states. The conflict between the two intensified in 1803 when Burr tied Jefferson in electoral votes for the presidency. In a runoff election, Hamilton used his influence to get Burr defeated. He succeeded. Jefferson became president, Burr, the vice president.

When Burr was nominated for governor of New York, Hamilton again engineered his defeat, by making statements of a negative nature about Burr's character. The result of this ideological struggle between Aaron Burr and Alexander Hamilton came to a climax in 1804 when a final insult became too much for Burr. Burr challenged Hamilton to a duel in New Jersey and fatally wounded him. And so, the Vice-President of the United States shot the first Secretary of the Treasury and the young country lost the services of two of its most outstanding men.

Hamilton dying after being shot.

American
Stock Exchange

11:57:36

PROFITABILITY IN THE THIRD QUARTER.
THE PREDICTED PROFIT IN THE THIRD QUARTER
WOULD BE THE FIRST QUARTERLY PROFIT FOR THE
COMPANY IN MORE THAN TWO YEARS.
CULLINANE ALSO SAID THE COMPANY'S GOAL IS
TO HAVE $50 MILLION IN RE

Brokers on the floor of the Exchange must constantly keep up with new information.

HOW THE STOCK MARKET WORKS TODAY

lthough the NYSE is the largest exchange, it is not the only game in town. In addition, there is the American Stock Exchange, or AMEX, the regional and foreign exchanges, and the over-the-counter, or OTC, market. Each one plays an important role on Wall Street.

The New York Stock Exchange

If you've ever visited the NYSE or watched scenes of the trading floor on television, you may have thought you were watching a circus. Many people at first find it noisy, exciting, and disorganized. Noisy and exciting, yes—but disorganized, no. The trading floor, often referred to simply as the **floor**, is about the size of a football field. It has hundreds of stockbrokers, clerks, and other men and women watching computer screens, answering the phones,

Floor: The area of an exchange where stocks are bought and sold.

35

and shouting out orders. Yet they all know precisely what they and their colleagues are doing.

Who Can Trade. To buy and sell securities on the floor of the exchange, one must first meet tough personal and financial standards and be accepted for membership. The number of memberships (or seats) is limited to 1,366. The price of a seat is based on supply and demand. During the 1977 recession, seats were as low as $35,000. In 1987 a record for the most expensive seat was set at $1,150,000.

Floorbroker: A broker who buys and sells stocks directly on the floor of the exchange of which he or she is a member.

There are several types of members. **Floorbrokers** make up the largest group. There are two types within this category: commission brokers and independent brokers.

Commission brokers are employed by brokerage firms that are members of the exchange. They travel from their booth to the trading posts, buying and selling securities for the public.

Independent floorbrokers work for themselves and handle orders for brokerage firms that do not have full-time brokers or whose brokers are too busy to handle a specific order. They are also called "$2 brokers," an old phrase referring to the days when they earned $2 for every 100 shares they traded.

A member firm is a brokerage firm that has membership on the exchange. The membership technically may be in the name of an officer or partner at the firm, not the firm itself.

Specialist: A stockbroker who handles specific stocks on the floor of an exchange. He or she is the person other members go to when they want to buy or sell these particular stocks.

Allied members are general partners or voting stockholders of a member firm of the exchange. They are not personally members. Allied members cannot do business on the trading floor.

A **specialist** is an exchange member who is an expert in several stocks and who trades only in those stocks. He or she is the person other members

SIGNIFICANT DAYS ON THE NYSE: MARKET HIGHS AND LOWS

March 16, 1830	Dullest day in history of the NYSE—31 shares traded
December 15, 1886	First million-share day—1,200,000 shares traded
October 23, 1907	**Call money** at 125 percent; Panic of 1907
October 29, 1929	The great stock market crash; start of the Depression
August 18, 1982	First 100 million-share day—132,681,120 shares traded
September 21, 1987	Highest price paid for a seat—$1,150,000
October 19, 1987	Largest drop in the **Dow Jones Industrial Average**: 508 points
October 20, 1987	Highest volume day—608,148,710 shares traded
October 13, 1989	Dow Jones Industrial Average plunged 190 points, second largest drop in history

go to when they wish to buy or sell one of those particular stocks. If, for example, there are no buyers for Reebok when you want to sell your shares, the specialist is required by the NYSE to offer Reebok shares from his own account to the floorbroker.

The specialist system began quite by accident in 1875 when James Boyd, an exchange member, broke his leg and was unable to move about the floor. Confined to one spot, he limited his trading to a single stock—Western Union— until his leg healed. To Boyd's surprise, his business actually increased as fellow brokers left orders with him when they wanted to buy or sell above or below the

Call money: The rate banks charge brokers for money loaned.

Dow Jones Industrial Average®: *An average of 30 actively traded well-known stocks that reflects their price changes.*

current price. Soon others on the floor also began specializing.

The exchange itself does not buy, sell, own, or set the prices of stocks traded on the floor. It is a quasi-public institution governed by the board of directors made up of twelve public representatives, twelve exchange members, and a full-time paid chairman, executive vice-chairman, and president.

At the end of 1989, 2,246 stocks were listed with 82.8 billion shares outstanding, having a value of $3 trillion. The number of companies listed was 1,721.

The American Stock Exchange

The American Stock Exchange (AMEX) has the second largest volume of trading in the United States. It is located near the NYSE, at 86 Trinity Place in New York. Until 1953 it was known as the Curb Exchange.

In general, the stocks traded on the AMEX are those of companies smaller than those on the NYSE. Although traditionally small-to-medium-sized companies traded first on the AMEX and then moved to the NYSE as they gained in size, this is no longer always the case. A number of companies prefer the atmosphere of the AMEX, which offers more personalized attention.

At the end of 1989, 1,057 issues were listed, with 8,902,572,115 shares outstanding, worth $132,562,206,567. The number of companies listed was 859.

The Over-the-Counter Market

Even though the NYSE and AMEX capture most of the attention, the majority of U.S. stocks are traded over the counter, through an electronic marketplace. The OTC market is not a physical place; traders do not meet on the floor of an exchange. Instead, they use computers to get the necessary information about prices and then buy and sell securities by telephone with other brokers. This network is called the National Market System, or NMS.

There are many OTC stocks that are not part of the NMS. Information about these stocks is given in the ***Pink Sheets,*** a daily publication printed on pink-colored paper, that is put out by the National Quotation Bureau. It gives the **bid and asked price** for thousands of OTC stocks, many of which are not listed in the financial newspapers. The pink sheets also give the names and telephone numbers of firms that trade each stock.

In the newspaper, OTC stocks are listed under the abbreviation NASDAQ, which stands for National Association of Security Dealers Automated Quotations. Because there are thousands of OTC stocks, far too many to list every day in the paper, only the most actively traded are listed.

OTC stocks are generally those of smaller companies that do not meet the more rigorous listing requirements of the NYSE or the AMEX.

Pink Sheets: *A daily publication listing over-the-counter stocks not traded on the National Association of Securities Dealers Automated Quotations network. The list gives the names of the brokers who trade that particular stock plus the previous day's prices.*

Bid and asked price: The highest price someone is willing to pay for a stock is the bid price and the lowest price at which someone will sell is the asked. Combined, the bid and asked is called a quotation.

Specialists gather on the floor of the exchange to buy and sell.

With a complicated system of hand signals, commodity traders on the Tokyo exchange communicate their bids.

The Regional Exchanges

A handful of small regional exchanges are located in major cities. They list regional or local stocks as well as many of the stocks listed on the NYSE and AMEX. This dual listing widens the market for individual stocks and also increases the number of hours when a stock can be traded.

Through the Intermarket Trading System (ITS), a video-computer system, eight of the markets are linked together: New York, American, Boston, Cincinnati, Midwest, Philadelphia, Pacific, and NASD. ITS enables brokers on the floor of any one of these exchanges to see the prices for the listed securities on several exchanges. A broker can then send an order to one of these exchanges, should the price be more favorable than on his own exchange.

Foreign Markets

Electronic technology has so shrunk the world that the global financial community never goes to sleep. At any hour of the day or night, somewhere a stock market is open, with traders buying and selling securities at a frenetic pace. In Europe the leading exchanges are located in London, Paris, and Frankfurt. In the Far East, Tokyo, Hong Kong, and Singapore lead the way. The trading results of these major stock exchanges are published daily in *The Wall Street Journal* under the heading "Stock Market Indexes." In the example below, the Zurich exchange was up over the previous day, while the Hong Kong exchange was closed.

The world's newest stock exchanges are in China. Before the communist takeover, the Shanghai Stock Exchange was one of the largest in the world. Then, in 1949, the Communists, who

Stock Market Indexes

EXCHANGE	8/28/89 CLOSE	NET CHG	PCT CHG
Tokyo Nikkei Average	34607.41	− 132.52	− 0.38
Tokyo Topix Index	2610.29	− 12.41	− 0.47
London FT 30-share	closed		
London 100-share	closed		
London Gold Mines	closed		
Frankfurt DAX	1595.87	− 8.51	− 0.53
Zurich Credit Suisse	679.7	+ .7	+ 0.10
Paris CAC General	523.2	+ .1	+ 0.02
Milan Stock Index	1233	+ 2	+ 0.16
Amsterdam ANP-CBS General	203.5	− 2.0	− 0.97
Stockholm Affarsvarlden	1335.2	− 8.2	− 0.61
Brussels Stock Index	6510.77	+ 21.25	+ 0.33
Australia All Ordinaries	1769.1	+ 3.9	+ 0.22
Hong Kong Hang Seng	closed		
Singapore Straits Times	1345.96	− 9.22	− 0.68
Johannesburg J'burg Gold	1600	− 15.0	− 0.93
Toronto 300 Composite	3968.11	-6.57	− 0.17
Euro, Aust, Far East MSCI-p	964.8	− 8.90	− 0.91

p-Preliminary
na-Not available

Trading Around The Clock, Around The World

Keyed to Eastern daylight time. Local hours shown next to each session.

PM		AM	AM	AM		PM	PM
9	MIDNIGHT	3	6	9	NOON	3	6

CLOSED

CLOSED

SOURCE:THE NEW YORK TIMES/OCT.16, 1989

viewed stocks as a tool of capitalism, shut down the exchange. All stocks and bonds were forbidden until 1986 when, in a move toward westernization, the government allowed several securities to be sold in Shenyang, a northern industrial city. Thousands of Chinese lined up outside the Shenyang exchange the night before, eager to participate in the "new capitalism." Many came in from the surrounding farms and villages on their bicycles, while those who lived closer walked to the tiny exchange. Their pockets were crammed with money they had hidden from the government for years.

Today small exchanges, open only a few hours a week, operate in Beijing, Shanghai, and Shenyang, selling just a handful of stocks. Chinese stocks are not available to foreigners.

JOHN J. PHELAN, JR.

John J. Phelan, Jr. presided over the New York Stock Exchange as its chairman during six years of extraordinary growth and turmoil. A consumate diplomat, he rose from a summer job on the Exchange floor to being a leader in the American financial world.

Phelan was the ideal person to lead the Exchange into the 1990s: he possessed the political and personal skills necessary to move the old-line floor traders into the age of the computer. A former floor trader himself, Phelan knew how to protect their interests and at the same time convince them of the much needed changes.

Phelan held his first Wall Street job at age 16, working for his father's specialist firm during summer vacations. He hated the experience, especially the noisy, shoving crowd and the gruff traders. "I told my father, 'I don't know what I'm going to do with my life, but I'm not going to work on Wall Street.'"

Yet in 1955, at the age of 23, after graduating magna cum laude from Adelphi University, he returned to the floor to work as a specialist trader. (Specialists market, or handle, particular stocks on the floor of the Exchange.) In 1971, his career took a slight change as he became a member of the Board of Governors of the Exchange. In 1975 he became vice chairman, a position he held until 1980.

Phelan, unlike many on Wall Street, foresaw the

John J. Phelan, Jr.

enormous growth in trading that was to come: in 1979, when the volume was 20 million shares, he told the Exchange it must prepare for 50 million. When he became chairman, he convinced the Board to spend millions of dollars on high-tech computerized systems so that large volumes of buy and sell orders could be handled.

Phelan, however, will probably best be remembered for his actions on October 19, 1987, when the Dow Jones Industrial Average fell an unprecedented 508 points. Members of the Exchange, many of whom were near panic, felt relieved and even hopeful when they saw Phelan appear, after a day of tumultuous trading, on a small balcony that overlooks the trading floor. His appearance there bespoke calm and assurance. That night on television, he told the world that the stock market was still in operation and would open the next morning. Although October 19 was one of the worst days on Wall Street, it was John Phelan's shining hour. He went on to provide a new type of leadership as the financial community recovered from the disaster, spending hours in Washington, appearing at Congressional panels, speaking to politicians and lawmakers, seeking answers to tough issues of the day: program trading, insider trading and giant corporate takeovers—topics many in the industry preferred to avoid.

Traders at Prudential Bache Securities, a brokerage firm on Wall Street, take orders from investors who want to buy and sell stocks.

4

YOUR BROKERAGE ACCOUNT

N ow that your know how the stock exchanges work, we can see how Reebok stock is actually bought and sold. In our Reebok story, the company has gone public and its shares are being traded on the NYSE. In the initial public offering, when Reebok shares were first sold to the public, the price was $14 per share. Now the price is no longer fixed. It is determined by supply and demand: the more investors who want to own Reebok shares and the fewer who want to sell it, the higher the price. The price changes many times a day. When you purchase a share of Reebok, you are betting that other investors will also want to buy the stock so your shares will rise in price.

In order to buy Reebok, you must first open a brokerage account, which is a process similar to opening a bank account. You cannot write or call the company to buy its stock. You must use a broker. The term *broker* comes from the French *brochier*, meaning one that broached, or tapped, a wine keg. Later on, the term was used to describe retailers who bought wine by the barrel and sold it to customers by the cup from a tap.

How to Pick a Stockbroker

Although the perfect stockbroker, just like the perfect parent or brother or sister, is difficult to define, you can find a broker you enjoy working with if you use common sense and ask a lot of questions. If you are still a minor (under age 18 or 21, depending upon the state you live in), you will have to open an account with your parent's help. But no matter how old you are, the techniques for finding a top-notch broker are the same.

Begin by asking other members of your family, your family lawyer, or accountant to recommend several candidates. Your local banker or one of your teachers may also have a broker. After you have three or four names, call each one and set up a time to meet them in person. You will want to take an adult with you.

Draw up a list of questions to ask and take the list with you. Make enough copies so that you have one for each interview.

You, too, should be prepared to answer some questions. A good broker will want to know if you have ever invested before and whether you have a checking or savings account. If you are working, the broker will ask how much money you make. A well-trained broker also will ask what your financial goals are. You should think about this beforehand. Are you investing in the market for immediate income (in which case, you will want a dividend-paying stock) or are you willing to wait for results

QUESTIONS TO ASK YOUR BROKER CANDIDATES

- How long have you been a broker?
- How long have you been with this firm?
- Where did you receive your training?
- Do you have a minimum dollar requirement for investing?
- How do you feel about having a student as a client?
- Do you have any other students who are clients?
- How do you select stocks?
- How do you decide when to sell a stock?
- Do you consult with your clients before purchasing stocks for their account?
- Will you give me the names of three of your clients as references?
- What was your record last year versus the Dow Jones Industrial Average?
- How would you advise me to invest my money?
- May I see your commission rate schedule?

and invest for price appreciation? Your broker should take the time to discuss these choices and to answer your questions.

After you have met with several brokers, compare the answers you received. You want to select a broker who is experienced, honest, trustworthy, and competent. Remember, this man or woman is going to be advising you on how to handle your money.

Whatever you do, don't use a broker who (1) refuses to provide you with references; (2) uses words you don't understand and then doesn't explain them to you when you ask; (3) makes you feel uneasy; (4) promises to make you very rich.

Full-Service Firms

The names of the larger national brokerage firms may already be familiar to you through their ads on

TV or in the newspapers. Or you may have passed their offices in your business district. The firm with the most customers is Merrill Lynch. It has 470 offices and 11,000 brokers.

There are two types of brokerage firms, full service and discount.

A full-service firm provides customers with research and advice on which stocks to buy. It charges higher commissions than the discount firm, which simply places buy and sell orders and does not help customers with investment decisions.

Using a Discount Broker

Discount firms are no-frills operations that merely handle buy and sell orders. Their commissions are 50 percent to 80 percent less than those charged by full-service firms. They can charge so much less because they do less for you. They have streamlined operations, fewer staff members, and no teams of **analysts**, researchers, or **portfolio managers** to help clients manage their investments.

Analyst: A person who evaluates a company's financial condition and determines whether it is a good investment.

Discount brokers are best for investors who know exactly what they want to buy or sell and do not need advice from a professional. For example, if you know you want stock of Apple Computer, then use a discount firm and save on the commission.

Portfolio manager: An expert responsible for building and overseeing the securities portfolio (a holding of more than one stock, bond, commodity, or other security) of an individual or institutional investor. Portfolio managers work for mutual funds, pension funds, and wealthy private investors.

Discount brokers advertise in the financial pages of most newspapers and are listed in the yellow pages of the phone book. Although there is no particular need to interview a discount broker, since you, not the broker, will be managing your money, it is a good idea to call several in your area and compare commission rates, noting any differences between minimums. With a discount firm, most contact is by phone, so select one that has plenty of people to respond to your buy and sell orders.

Many large banks offer a discount brokerage service through a **subsidiary**. You may find it more convenient to do business with your bank.

Subsidiary: A company controlled or owned by another company; the latter is known as the parent company.

Among the leading national discount brokerage firms are:
•Fidelity
Boston, MA
800-225-1799; in MA: 800-882-1269
•Quick & Reilly
New York, NY
800-221-5220; in NY: 800-522-8712
•Charles Schwab
San Francisco, CA
800-648-5300; in CA: 800-792-0988

How to Open a Brokerage Account

Once you and your parents have decided on a broker, the next step is to open an account. It's not difficult, but you will have to provide the information required by the New York Stock Exchange's Rule 405, the "Know Your Customer" rule. This states that a broker should know enough about a client to make intelligent, suitable investment recommendations for him or her.

You will probably be asked to supply some or all of these facts:
•Name
•Address
•Social security number
•Telephone number
•Employer's name and address
•Bank accounts and numbers
•Personal references
•Proof of age if you are a minor

• Previous and existing brokerage accounts
• Name of person who referred you to the broker or firm
• How dividends and interest income are to be handled–invested by the firm in a money market or sent to you
• Whether your stocks are to be held **"in street name"** for you by the broker, or sent to you

In street name: Securities held in the broker's custody and not the customer's possession, making transfer of shares when sold easier.

If you are a minor, your account will be opened under the Uniform Gifts to Minors Act (UGMA). This law, adopted by most states, sets up rules for handling assets placed in the name of an adult as **custodian** for a child. Often, the custodian is a parent but can be someone else. Securities are placed in a Uniform Gifts to Minors account. When you legally become an adult, these assets are yours to do with as you please.

Custodian: An organization, typically a bank, or a person, who holds in custody the assets (stocks, bonds, cash, etc.) for someone else, often a minor.

Legally the custodian has the right to determine how the money is invested. However, if you are investing your own money and if you are trying to learn how to handle this money, it is important that you be allowed to make some of the decisions.

There are several other types of accounts brokerage firms offer. You should know about them for the future.

• *A joint account.* This type of account can be opened by any two individuals. They do not have to be married or even related. There are two types of joint accounts. The more common type of joint account is a "joint tenancy with rights of survivorship." In this type of account, if one account holder dies, the other receives all the assets. Because the assets bypass **probate** and go directly to the survivor, this is sometimes known as "the poor man's will." A variation of this type of account is "tenancy

Probate: A legal process in which the will of a deceased person is presented to a court and an administrator is appointed to fulfill the terms of the will.

in entirety" for married couples, in which the husband or wife automatically acquires the other's share upon death.

You may also have a "tenancy in common" account, in which the survivor does not receive the deceased's share of the account. That property goes to the deceased's heirs. The survivor must then open a new account.

• *Discretionary account.* This type of account requires special written authorization as well as approval by an officer or partner of the brokerage firm. In a discretionary account, you give your broker discretion or the right to buy and sell securities *without* consulting you ahead of time.

TYPES OF ORDERS

Market order: Tells the broker to buy or sell at the best price currently available.

Limit order : Tells the broker to buy or sell at a specific price or better—lower for buying or higher for selling.

GTC: "Good 'til cancelled" tells the broker to buy or sell at a specified price until the investor cancels the order.

Round lot: Tells the broker to buy or sell stock in units of 100 shares.

Stop order: Tells the broker to buy or sell at the market price once the stock has traded at a stated price, called the stop price. For example, you buy 100 shares of Reebok at $10 per share. It goes to $20. You feel this is as high as it will go, so you give your broker a stop order at $17. If Reebok continues to go up in price, the broker won't sell. If it falls to $17, he must sell as close as possible to $17.

This type of account should be opened only if you have complete trust in your broker, or if you are going to be out of the country for some time.

• *A margin account.* This type of account allows you to borrow money in order to purchase securities. You must sign a special loan consent to open a margin account. This consent pledges your stocks as **collateral**. Your stocks must be held in street name in a margin account, which means the brokerage firm, not you, keeps the stock certificates.

Collateral: An asset pledged to a lender until a loan is repaid. If the borrower doesn't pay back the loan, the lender can sell the collateral to pay off the loan.

A Trading Day in Reebok Stock

Once you have opened a brokerage account, you can place your own order for Reebok stock, either by telephone or in person. It will resemble the following example, although each brokerage firm's procedures vary slightly. In reality, larger orders follow these steps; smaller orders are sent directly to the specialist's post.

•*Wednesday, 8:30 A.M.* You check the financial pages of the newspaper for Reebok International before going to school. You find the price and other data listed under the heading "New York Stock Exchange Composite Trading." The closing price on Tuesday was $14 per share.

•*9:45 A.M.* You call your stockbroker before first period and tell him you're interested in buying shares of Reebok. He punches in the **stock symbol** for Reebok (RBK) on his desktop quotation machine and reads off the price. The bid and asked price as well as the last sale price will flash on the screen. (Bid is the highest

Stock symbol: Letters used to identify a stock on the ticker tape or video display terminals. For example, "C" is for Chrysler, "SPP" for Scott Paper Company.

price a buyer will pay; asked is the lowest price acceptable to a seller.) The stock is offered at 14 1/4. You decide to buy 75 shares because that comes to just over $1,000, within your budget. But your broker advises you to buy a **round lot**, or 100 shares. This is the standard unit of trade and the commission will be proportionately less than for an odd lot. An odd lot is anything under 100 shares.

Round lot: The standard unit of trading stocks—100 shares.

You give your broker a **market order** to buy 100 shares of Reebok. Although there are a number of different types of orders, this is the most common. It tells the broker to buy (or sell) at the best price currently available in the market. It's offered at 14 1/4. This is the lowest (asked price) at which anyone would sell. You place a market order for 100 shares of Reebok. The exact price is not guaranteed, but the sale takes place as soon as possible. (The market opens in New York at 9:30 A.M.)

Market order: An order to buy or sell a stock as soon as possible at the best possible price.

•*10:00* A.M. Your broker fills out an order form, which includes:
1. Your account number
2. The stock exchange
3. The stock symbol
4. Number of shares
5. Type of order
6. The broker's number
7. Whether you are buying or selling
8. Whether it is a solicited or an unsolicited order

•*10:11* A.M. The order is given to the firm's order clerk, who immediately enters it into a computer.

Reading the Ticker Tape

s The number preceding the letter s should be multiplied by 100 to get the number of shares traded. Any number over 10,000 is correct at face value.

Top row This is where the stock symbols are listed.

Pr This is the symbol for preferred stock.

BP   FBC   AMXPrB   ASPr   TX

$24\frac{3}{4}$ $6\frac{7}{8}$ $9\frac{1}{4}$ $25s40\frac{1}{2}$ $5s21\frac{5}{8}$ $200{.}000s4$

Bottom row This is where the volume or number of shares traded and the price per share are given. The volume appears first. If no volume number precedes the price, the transaction was for 100 shares, that is, for a round lot. For example, 100 shares of FBC were sold at 9 1/4. However, the number listed is not always the actual price. In order to accurately read the tape, you *must* be familiar with a stock's trading range. When a high–priced stock lists a number under 10, it means that the number listed must be *added* to the low end of the stock's $10 trading range. The trading range is always defined in units of $10.

•**10:16 A.M.** The order is transmitted by computer to the firm's booth on the floor of the New York Stock Exchange where Reebok shares are bought and sold. Your brokerage firm's floortrader takes the order to the specialist's post where Reebok is traded.The specialist is a member of the exchange and trades Reebok stock as well as several other stocks. Each stock listed on the NYSE is traded at one of the specialist's posts. The specialist remains at that post while the market is open.

•**10:21 A.M.** The floorbroker asks the specialist for details on the market in Reebok, at the same time checking the video screen for the last price, which was $14 per share.

•**10:22 A.M.** The specialist says: "$14 to 1/4, 100, 200." This means there are 100 shares bid for, and 200 shares offered for sale.

•**10:24 A.M.** A crowd is gathering at the Reebok post and there are several other bids in at $14 because of interest in the company, so your broker wants to move your buy order quickly. He bids 14 1/8 by calling out: "14 1/8 for 100."

Block trade This is a trade of over 10,000 shares of stock.

& The letter following the ampersand symbolizes the exchange where the trade took place.

LAST This signifies that this was the last trade of the day for this company.

MX UNP C GLW PHH HAL ICN&N▪LAST

$6\frac{1}{8}$ 5 $4\frac{3}{4}$ 6 $6\frac{7}{8}$ $5\frac{3}{8}$ $1\frac{1}{8}$▪▪▪ 24

- **10:24 and 2 seconds:** Neither the specialist nor any other broker in the crowd responds, which means the bid is not accepted.

- **10:25 A.M.** Your broker bids higher, "I'll take 100 at 1/4."

- **10:26 A.M.** The specialist shouts: "Sold." Both men write the details of the sale in their books, but no papers actually exchange hands. After the trade for Reebok is made, a reporter or recorder puts a computer card into a reporting machine and the trade immediately appears on the **ticker tape**. The electronic ticker tape, which records each trade immediately, is displayed on the trading floor and on quote-machine screens in brokerage offices across the nation.

- **10:29 A.M.** The purchase of 100 shares of Reebok is reported back to your brokerage firm by computer. This is called a confirmation. The purchase is also entered into your account by the same electronic system that reports the transaction to the exchange's ticker tape, an electronic tape that runs all day long, recording the current prices of all the stocks as the trades are made on the exchange.

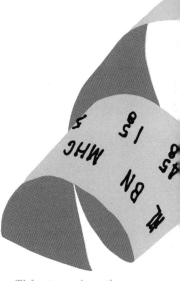

Ticker tape: A continuous roll of narrow paper on which stock transactions were printed before the computer age. Today the "tape," with the stock symbol followed by the latest price, is electronically produced.

•*10:32* A.M. After several more trades of Reebok at prices of 14 1/8, 14 1/4, and 14 3/8, the price reaches 14 1/2. The tape is updated each time.

•*4:00* P.M. Your stockbroker calls your house. He leaves a message on the answering machine that your order has been executed and asks that you call him at home for the details.

•*6:45* P.M. You return home and call your broker. He explains that you purchased 100 shares of Reebok at 14 1/4. He gives you the settlement date—the date on which the stock must be paid for. He also tells you he has mailed you a confirmation slip indicating the name of the stock, the price at which it was bought, the number of shares, the settlement date, and the date the transaction took place.

•*7:00* P.M. You listen to the "Nightly Business News" on public television and learn that Reebok closed the day at 15 1/2, up 1 1/2 points from the closing price of the previous day.

Thursday. You receive the confirmation slip in the mail. You write a check, made out to the brokerage firm with your account number on the face of the check, paying the total amount, including commission. You mail the check that evening to make certain it will reach your broker by settlement date, which is five business days after the purchase of your Reebok stock.

CONGRATULATIONS! You have taken the first steps toward building your investment portfolio.

Smaller orders do not take this many steps to complete. They are sent directly to the specialist's computer and the trade is made electronically through the Designated Order Turnaround, or DOT, system.

The Role of the Specialist

What would have happened if no one wanted to sell their Reebok shares when you wanted to buy? This is where the specialist gets involved. Every stock is traded at one specific location on the floor of the exchange. (See diagram below.) Like all stocks, Reebok has a specialist assigned to it. The specialist

Floorplan of the New York Stock Exchange Trading Floor

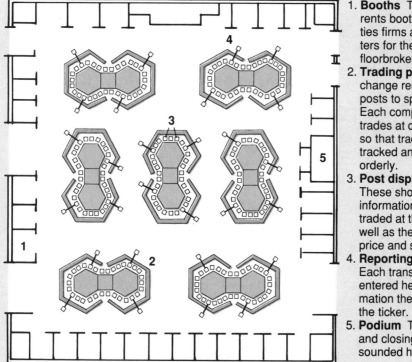

1. **Booths** The exchange rents booths to securities firms as headquarters for the firm's floorbrokers.
2. **Trading posts** The exchange rents these posts to specialist firms. Each company's stock trades at only one post so that trading can be tracked and kept orderly.
3. **Post display units** These show the day's information on stocks traded at that post as well as the last sale price and size of order.
4. **Reporting device** Each transaction is entered here. The information then registers on the ticker.
5. **Podium** The opening and closing bell is sounded here.

owns shares of Reebok in his own account and he uses those shares when necessary—when there are more buyers than sellers or vice versa.

If your broker cannot fill your order at once because there are no sellers at that time, he leaves the order with the specialist at the specialist's post. The specialist keeps a list of buy and sell orders for Reebok stock that have been placed by other brokers. He then tries to match buy and sell orders as the day proceeds. In this way, the specialist acts as a broker for other brokers, filling their orders. He charges them a commission when he fills an order.

If there were no sellers of Reebok when you wanted to buy, you still would have made your purchase. The floorbroker would have bought the stock for you from the specialist's own account.

The specialist or his firm is required to have in capital $4 million to operate. This was increased from only $100,000 because of problems encountered in the 1987 market crash.

What to Do with Your Stock Certificate

Almost the only piece of paper involved in the Reebok transaction is the stock certificate.

• *In street name.* Most investors do not physically take possession of their stock certificates. Instead, they have their ownership recorded electronically in their brokerage account. This enables you to sell your stock more quickly in the future. It also protects you against loss of the certificate.

When certificates are held in street name, the firm collects the dividends and either sends them to you directly or puts them in your money market fund at the firm. In addition, quarterly and annual reports and any proxy statements are also sent to you through your broker.

• ***Keeping your certificates.*** If you want to, you can have your stockbroker mail the certificate to you. It will be sent by a **transfer agent**, usually a bank appointed by the corporation to maintain its stock records, and to issue new certificates. In your financial notebook, record the certificate number, the price at which the stock was purchased, the number of shares, and the commission. Leave space to record dividend payments, stock splits, and price changes. Then immediately place the certificates in your safe-deposit box at the bank.

Transfer agent: An agent, usually a bank, selected by a corporation to keep its records of stock owners, to cancel and issue new certificates when stocks are sold, and to handle lost or stolen certificates. (A corporation can be its own transfer agent.)

• ***Selling your stock.*** You can, of course, sell your shares through your broker. If you are holding the certificate, you must deliver it to your broker, either in person or by registered mail. Before you turn over the certificate, record the certificate numbers and the number of shares involved.

If you sell your stock, you are responsible for keeping track of capital gains or losses made when you sell. This dollar amount must be reported to the Internal Revenue Service on your personal tax return. The company sends you a tax form recording the number of shares sold and at what price, but it's up to you to know the price at which you bought the shares. This should have been recorded in your financial notebook.

• ***Registering ownership of your stock.*** It's best to use exactly the same form of name and address for all stock transactions. Don't register one certificate in the name of Samantha A. Campbell and another in the name of S.A. Campbell. It only causes confusion.

You can also give or transfer your stock to someone else. Your broker will tell you how. When you become of legal age, your custodian should change the registration on your account to your name. Again, check with your broker.

Tracking Your Stocks

In order to know whether to keep your stock, buy more shares, or sell it, you must keep track of its price and dividends. Use this sample worksheet for this purpose and keep it in your financial notebook. Make enough photocopies so that you will have one for each stock you own.

Name of corporation:

_____

_____Common _____ Preferred

Purchased from:

Broker:_____

Address:_____

Telephone:_____

Where certificates are held:

_____

_____

_____

Purchases:

Date of Purchase	No. of shares	Price per share	Total $ commission	Value on 12/31

Sales

Date sold	No. of shares sold	Price per share	$ profit/loss

Dividend Income

Date	Amount

Stock Splits

Date	New number of shares owned	Price per share at time of split

What About Your Dividends?

Record date: Date on
which a share-
holder must own a
company's stock in
order to receive its
next dividend. For
example, the board
of directors may
vote a dividend
payable March 1 to
shareholders of
record on February
15.

Payment date: Date on
which a declared
stock dividend will
be paid to share-
holders of record.

Ex-dividend: Time period
between the an-
nouncement and
the payment of a
stock's dividend.
An investor who
buys the stock
during this interval
does not receive the
dividend. (Ex
means without).

If your stocks are in street name, your broker will receive all dividend checks and forward them to you or put them into your brokerage account. If you personally hold your certificates, then you will receive the checks. Companies establish a **record date**, or the date on which a shareholder must own the stock in order to receive the next dividend payment. In most cases, the record date is several weeks in advance of the dividend **payment date**. However, to allow for bookkeeping procedures, an **ex-dividend date** governs the dividend rights of purchasers and sellers. The ex-dividend date is the fourth business day preceding the record date. After the ex-dividend date, the stock is sold "ex," or without its dividend. For example, if a stock is sold prior to the ex-dividend date, the purchaser is entitled to the dividend. But if the stock is sold on or after the ex-dividend date, the purchaser is not entitled to the dividend. A tiny "x" will be printed next to the stock's name in the stock tables in the newspaper on the first day on which a buyer cannot receive the dividend.

Usually you will receive a dividend check approximately every three months. You should record the date on which your dividend check normally arrives.

You must report dividends as income when you file your personal tax return. At the end of the year, the company will send you an IRS Form 1099, which lists all dividends paid during the year.

JAY GOULD AND BLACK FRIDAY

September 24, 1869, is known in stock market annals as Black Friday. On this infamous day, thousands of gold speculators were ruined in a financial panic, all due to the daring manipulations of the market by one of its most audacious speculators, thirty-three-year-old Jay Gould.

Gould's most outrageous scheme was his attempt to corner the nation's entire gold market at the end of the Civil War. He almost succeeded.

During the Civil War, the United States had issued millions of dollars in paper money, called greenbacks. Since the greenbacks were not redeemable in gold, people hoarded the precious metal and it soon became scarce. Gold sold at a premium while greenbacks were worth far less than their face value.

At the same time, the government had nearly $80 million in gold in its Treasury. It was generally believed that President Grant would sell the government's gold in the public market to bring its price back down to normal levels and to prevent further hoarding. Gould, who already owned $15 million of gold, wanted to convince Grant that a higher price would be good for the country. In the meantime, Gould purchased large quantities of gold at $130 an ounce, putting some in his friend Able Corbin's name, who was brother-in-law to President Grant, with the understanding that Corbin did not have to pay for it until it was sold. Gould thought that with Corbin involved in the scheme, the President wouldn't sell. But when the price went out of sight, pressure from other sources built up and President Grant decided it was in the best interest of the country to sell the government's gold.

Gould learned of the President's decision from Corbin and the two men conspired to keep the facts from the public. Knowing that the end was near, Gould then convinced his trusted associate, James Fisk, to buy gold to keep the price up so Gould could sell his millions near the top of the market. Fisk did just that, buying and raising the price from $145 to $160 while Gould's people quietly sold.

On September 24, when the news hit Wall Street that Washington was going to sell, brokers went wild trying to dump their holdings. But it was too late. The price fell rapidly and gold closed that day at $135. Gould, of course, had already dumped his supply at the top of the market, at $160.

A Congressional hearing followed and there was an endless stream of lawsuits against Gould, but he was never convicted.

Jay Gould

The computer room of the New York Stock Exchange contains billions of bits of information.

5

TAKING THE MARKET'S PULSE

N ow that you own shares of Reebok stock, you want to know its progress, whether it is moving up or down in price. One way is to check the financial pages of your daily newspaper.

How to Read the Financial Pages

When you open the newspaper to the listing of stock prices for the first time, it looks like a maze of numbers in tiny type. It's not as overwhelming as it appears. There is one simple rule to keep in mind as you read the tables: stock prices are quoted in fractions of a dollar: 5 3/4 is equal to $5.75; 5 1/2 means $5.50; 5 1/4 is $5.25; 5 1/8 equals $5.125. The example on the next page, taken from *The Wall Street Journal*, shows the listing for Reebok on the New York Stock Exchange. The American Stock

Exchange has a separate listing. Your local newspaper may use other headings and arrange data in a slightly different order.

Reebok is in the R section of the listing.

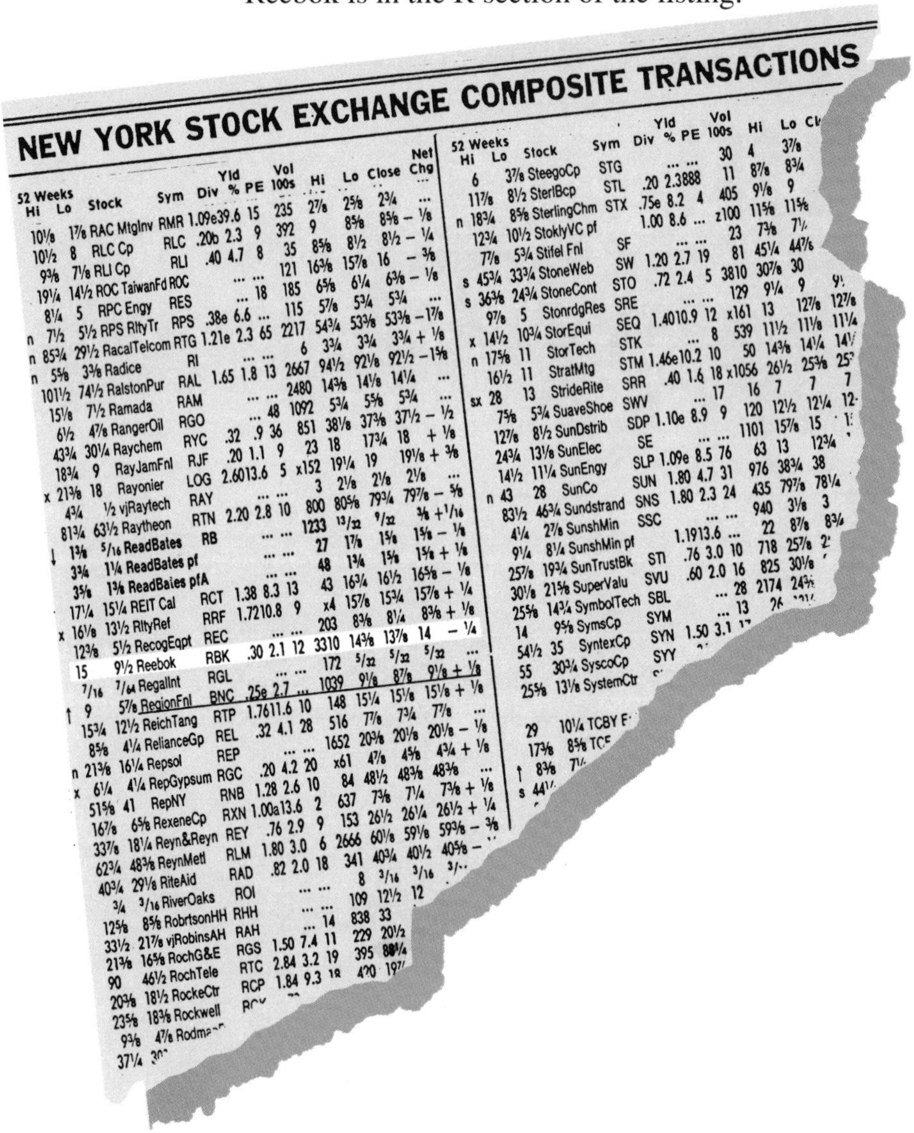

NEW YORK STOCK EXCHANGE COMPOSITE TRANSACTIONS

	52 Weeks Hi	52 Weeks Lo	Stock	Sym	Div	Yld %	PE	Vol 100s	Hi	Lo	Close	Net Chg
	10 1/8	1 7/8	RAC MtgInv	RMR	1.09e	39.6	15	235	2 7/8	2 5/8	2 3/4	...
	10 1/2	8	RLC Cp	RLC	.20b	2.3	9	392	9	8 5/8	8 5/8	- 1/8
	9 3/8	7 1/8	RLI Cp	RLI	.40	4.7	8	35	8 5/8	8 1/2	8 1/2	- 1/4
	19 1/4	14 1/2	ROC TaiwanFd	ROC		...	...	121	16 3/8	15 7/8	16	- 3/8
	8 1/4	5	RPC Engy	RES		...	18	185	6 5/8	6 1/4	6 3/8	- 1/8
n	7 1/2	5 1/2	RPS RltyTr	RPS	.38e	6.6	...	115	5 7/8	5 3/4	5 3/4	...
n	85 3/4	29 1/2	RacalTelcom	RTG	1.21e	2.3	65	2217	54 3/4	53 3/8	53 3/8	-1 7/8
n	5 5/8	3 3/8	Radice	RI		...	...	6	3 3/4	3 3/4	3 3/4	+ 1/8
	101 1/2	74 1/2	RalstonPur	RAL	1.65	1.8	13	2667	94 1/2	92 1/8	92 1/2	-1 5/8
	15 1/8	7 1/2	Ramada	RAM		...	...	2480	14 3/8	14 1/8	14 1/4	...
	6 1/2	4 7/8	RangerOil	RGO		...	48	1092	5 3/4	5 5/8	5 3/4	...
	43 3/4	30 1/4	Raychem	RYC	.32	.9	36	851	38 1/8	37 3/8	37 1/2	- 1/2
	18 3/4	9	RayJamFnl	RJF	.20	1.1	9	23	18	17 3/4	18	+ 1/8
x	21 3/8	18	Rayonier	LOG	2.60	13.6	5	x152	19 1/4	19	19 1/8	+ 3/8
	4 3/4	1/2	vjRaytech	RAY		...	...	3	2 1/8	2 1/8	2 1/8	...
	81 3/4	63 1/2	Raytheon	RTN	2.20	2.8	10	800	80 5/8	79 3/4	79 7/8	- 5/8
↓	1 3/8	5/16	ReadBates	RB		...	...	1233	13/32	9/32	3/8	+1/16
	3 3/4	1 1/4	ReadBates pf			...	...	27	1 7/8	1 5/8	1 5/8	- 1/8
	3 5/8	1 3/8	ReadBates pfA			...	...	48	1 3/4	1 5/8	1 5/8	+ 1/8
	17 1/4	15 1/4	REIT Cal	RCT	1.38	8.3	13	43	16 3/4	16 1/2	16 5/8	- 1/8
x	16 1/8	13 1/2	RltyRef	RRF	1.72	10.8	9	x4	15 7/8	15 3/4	15 7/8	+ 1/4
	12 3/8	5 1/2	RecogEqpt	REC		...	...	203	8 3/8	8 1/4	8 3/8	+ 1/8
	15	9 1/2	Reebok	RBK	.30	2.1	12	3310	14 3/8	13 7/8	14	- 1/4
	7/16	7/64	RegalInt	RGL		...	...	172	5/32	5/32	5/32	...
↑	9	5 7/8	RegionFnl	BNC	.25e	2.7	...	1039	9 1/8	8 7/8	9 1/8	+ 1/8
	15 3/4	12 1/2	ReichTang	RTP	1.76	11.6	10	148	15 1/4	15 1/8	15 1/8	+ 1/8
	8 5/8	4 1/4	RelianceGp	REL	.32	4.1	28	516	7 7/8	7 3/4	7 7/8	...
n	21 3/8	16 1/4	Repsol	REP		...	...	1652	20 3/8	20 1/8	20 1/8	- 1/8
x	6 1/4	4 1/4	RepGypsum	RGC	.20	4.2	20	x61	4 7/8	4 5/8	4 3/4	+ 1/8
	51 5/8	41	RepNY	RNB	1.28	2.6	10	84	48 1/2	48 3/8	48 3/8	...
	16 7/8	6 5/8	RexeneCp	RXN	1.00a	13.6	2	637	7 3/8	7 1/4	7 3/8	+ 1/8
	33 7/8	18 1/4	Reyn&Reyn	REY	.76	2.9	9	153	26 1/2	26 1/4	26 1/2	+ 1/4
	62 3/4	48 3/8	ReynMetl	RLM	1.80	3.0	6	2666	60 1/8	59 1/8	59 3/8	- 3/8
	40 3/4	29 1/8	RiteAid	RAD	.82	2.0	18	341	40 3/4	40 1/2	40 5/8	-
	3/4	3/16	RiverOaks	ROI		...	...	8	3/16	3/16	3/	
	12 5/8	8 5/8	RobrtsonHH	RHH		...	...	109	12 1/2	12		
	33 1/2	21 7/8	vjRobinsAH	RAH		...	14	838	33			
	21 3/8	16 5/8	RochG&E	RGS	1.50	7.4	11	229	20 1/2			
	90	46 1/2	RochTele	RTC	2.84	3.2	19	395	88 1/4			
	20 3/8	18 1/2	RockeCtr	RCP	1.84	9.3	18	420	19 7/			
	23 5/8	18 3/8	Rockwell	RC								
	9 3/8	4 7/8	Rodma									
	37 1/4	30										

	52 Weeks Hi	52 Weeks Lo	Stock	Sym	Div	Yld %	PE	Vol 100s	Hi	Lo	Cl
	6	3 7/8	SteegoCp	STG		...	...	30	4	3 7/8	
	11 7/8	8 1/2	SterlBcp	STL	.20	2.3	88	11	8 7/8	8 3/4	
n	18 3/4	8 5/8	SterlingChm	STX	.75e	8.2	4	405	9 1/8	9	
	12 3/4	10 1/2	StoklyVC pf		1.00	8.6	...	z100	11 5/8	11 5/8	
	7 7/8	5 3/4	Stifel Fnl	SF		...	...	23	7 3/8	7 1/	
s	45 3/4	33 3/4	StoneWeb	SW	1.20	2.7	19	81	45 1/4	44 7/8	
s	36 3/8	24 3/4	StoneCont	STO	.72	2.4	5	3810	30 7/8	30	
	9 7/8	5	StonrdgRes	SRE		...	...	129	9 1/4	9	9
x	14 1/2	10 3/4	StorEqui	SEQ	1.40	10.9	12	x161	13	12 7/8	12 7/8
n	17 5/8	11	StorTech	STK		...	8	539	11 1/2	11 1/8	11 1/4
	16 1/2	11	StratMtg	STM	1.46e	10.2	10	50	14 3/8	14 1/4	14 1/
sx	28	13	StrideRite	SRR	.40	1.6	18	x1056	26 1/2	25 3/8	25
	7 5/8	5 3/4	SuaveShoe	SWV		...	17	16	7	7	7
	12 7/8	8 1/2	SunDstrib	SDP	1.10e	8.9	9	120	12 1/2	12 1/4	12
	24 3/4	13 1/8	SunElec	SE		...	...	1101	15 7/8	15	1
	14 1/2	11 1/4	SunEngy	SLP	1.09e	8.5	76	63	13	12 3/4	
n	43	28	SunCo	SUN	1.80	4.7	31	976	38 3/4	38	
	83 1/2	46 3/4	Sundstrand	SNS	1.80	2.3	24	435	79 7/8	78 1/4	
	4 1/4	2 7/8	SunshMin	SSC		...	...	940	3 1/8	3	
	9 1/4	8 1/4	SunshMin pf		1.19	13.6	...	22	8 7/8	8 3/4	
	25 7/8	19 3/4	SunTrustBk	STI	.76	3.0	10	718	25 7/8	2	
	30 1/8	21 5/8	SuperValu	SVU	.60	2.0	16	825	30 1/8		
	25 5/8	14 3/4	SymbolTech	SBL		...	28	2174	24 3/		
	14	9 5/8	SymsCp	SYM		...	13	26			
	54 1/2	35	SyntexCp	SYN	1.50	3.1	1				
	55	30 3/4	SyscoCp	SYY							
	25 5/8	13 1/8	SystemCtr	S							
	29	10 1/4	TCBY E								
	17 3/8	8 5/8	TCF								
↑	8 3/8	7 1/									
s	44 1/										

- ***First and second colums:*** The highest and lowest prices for the past 52 weeks are given. If the stock has reached a new high or low for the year, this will be indicated by an arrow in the left hand margin. These 52-week figures indicate **price volatility**, often a sign of possible profit or loss.

Price volatility: The degree to which a stock's price has moved, either up or down.

Volatility, however, is relative: a $2 move in an $8 stock has greater impact than a $2 move in a $40 stock. In this example, Reebok moved $6.50—or, in the language of Wall Street, 6 1/2 points.

- **Third column**. *The company name* is abbreviated. Look carefully. Sometimes two companies have very similar names.
- **Fourth column.** The official stock symbol, the same one that appears on the ticker tape or which your broker uses in his quote machine. *Letter symbols* such as "pf" or "pr" indicate that the stock is preferred. If there are no such letters, it is a common stock. "Wt" following a company name indicates that the quotation is for a **warrant**, the right to buy the stock at a certain price for a certain period, usually from two to five years. The letter "S" indicates a recent stock split. "N" means a new stock, issued within the last 52 weeks.

Warrant: A type of security that allows the owner to buy a certain amount of common stock at a specified price for a limited time.

- **Fifth column.** The dividend column shows the *cash dividend per share*. The dividend is a payment of part of the company's profits to stockholders. The figure in the newspaper reflects the latest annual cash dividends. In the case of Reebok, the yearly dividend is 30 cents per share. If the dividend column is blank, the company isn't expected to pay a dividend.
- **Sixth column.** Yield is a way of stating the stock's current return on your investment. It is found by dividing the dividend by the price. It tells how much dividend shareholders receive at the current price. To determine the yield on your own, divide the dividend by the closing price. For Reebok's yield, divide 30 cents by 14 and you get 2.1 percent. The yield column is blank if there are no dividends.
- **Seventh column.** The *P-E Ratio*, which is an abbreviation for price-earnings ratio, expresses the relationship between the price of the stock and the

company's annual earnings; p = price and e = earnings. If the P/E is 10, that means the price of the stock is 10 times the company's earnings per share for the last four quarters. The P/E figure indicates the value of a stock in terms of the company's earnings, not in terms of its selling price. P/E ratios can be used to compare how expensive a stock is vis-a-vis its reported earnings. Unpopular stocks usually have low P/Es and popular stocks have high P/Es. Reebok's P/E is 12.

• *Eighth column.* *"Vol 100s"* means sales in hundreds, or the volume of shares traded on the prior day. Multiply the figure in the column by 100. For example, 331,000 shares of Reebok stock were traded. Occasionally, stocks with unusual sales volume are underlined in black. If the letter "z" appears before this number, it means you should not multiply by 100; the figure is the actual number of shares traded. Odd lots, or sales under 100 shares, are not listed.

• *Ninth to eleventh columns.* These next three figures tell a stock's *highest, lowest*, and *closing* price for the prior day. Reebok fluctuated from 13 7/8 to 14 3/8 and closed at 14.

• *Far right.* *Net change* illustrates the difference between the closing price for the day and the closing price of the prior day. A minus (-) sign indicates that the closing price is lower than that of the prior day; a plus (+) means it is higher. If a stock's price changed 5 percent or more, the figures are in bold type. Reebok closed down 1/4, or 25 cents, from the prior day.

Over-the-Counter Stocks

The financial pages for OTC stocks are slightly different than those for NYSE and AMEX issues.

OTC prices are given in three separate sections. First, turn to the heading "NASDAQ National Market Issues." This lists the most actively traded OTC stocks. Many of these stocks do not pay dividends because they are small, and are often new start-up companies that plow earnings back into the business.

For example, Aaron Rents pays an annual dividend of 10 cents for a yield of 0.8 percent. It closed the day up 1/8 at 13 1/2 but did not surpass its 52-week high of 15 1/4.

The second tier of OTC stocks are under the heading "NASDAQ Bid & Asked Quotations." Less data is given here—only the bid and asked prices and net change in price for the day—because these stocks are less actively traded. For example, Foliage Co. does not pay a dividend. It was bid at 3 1/8, the ask was 3 3/8, and the price was unchanged from the previous day.

NASDAQ BID & ASKED QUOTATIONS

Stock & Div	Sales 100s	Bid	Asked	Net Chg.
-A-A-A-				
ACSEn	3	1 7/16	1 9/16	...
AMR wt	26	253	262	− 1
APA s	39	8	8 3/4	− 1/4
ASK Cp	2130	13/32	7/16	+ 1/32
ATC	28	2 7/16	2 5/8	...
ATC wt	2	1 1/8	1 1/2	...
Abtx un	41	6	6 1/4	+ 3/8
AckCm h	268	8 3/4	9 1/4	+ 7/8
ActnSt s	2113	1 1/8	1 3/16	...
AdNMR	246	3 3/8	3 1/2	...
A NMR wt	123	2 1/4	2 5/8	− 1/16
AdvPr	106	2	2 1/8	−
AdPrd un	65	8 1/2	9 5/8	...
Aeroson	3	1 1/2	1 5/8	...
AirSen	125	1 5/8	1 11/16	+ 1/8
AirInt	213	2 5/16	2	...
Alcide	134	4 1/2	4 3/4	− 1/8
Alden .10e	32	1 13/16	1 15/16	− 1/16
Alphal	5	1 1/2	1 9/16	+ 1/8
AlsFrm	125	18	18 1/2	...
Amribc .20e	55	1 9/32	1 11/32	+ 1/32
AAcft	2125	15/16	1 1/8	...
AmBio	96	5 1/4	5 1/2	...
AmBdy	12	845	2 13/16	...

Stock & Div	Sales 100s	Bid	Asked	Net Chg.
FtMed	19	2 1/4	2 3/8	...
FNtOh	33	1 3/4	2	...
FRegBc	40	3 1/2	4 1/4	...
FUtdSv .30a	5	10 1/2	11 1/4	...
FishBu	230	2 1/2	3 1/4	...
FishTrn	120	11/16	13/16	− 1/16
Fisons .78e	292	22 1/4	22 3/8	− 1/8
Flexwat	5	1	1 1/8	...
Florfx	4	31/32	1 1/32	...
Foliage	235	3 1/8	3 3/8	...
Foreind	148	2 1/4	2 3/16	− 1/8
FrmRe .01e	50	9/32	11/32	...
Franch	85	15/16	1 1/2	...
FrntSvg	10	1 5/8	2 1/8	...
-G-G-G-				
GTEC Spf 1.00	65	11 3/4	11 3/4	+ 3/16
GTS	40	1 1/8	1 3/4	...
Galgph	24	2 3/8	2 7/8	+ 1/4
GnCom	338	5	5 1/8	...
GnMicro	45	7 3/4	9	...
GnScl	52	37 1/2	39	+ 1 1/2
GenesCp 1.20a	10	13/16	7/8	...
GenetEn				
Geotek				

Stock & Div	Sales 100s	Bid	Asked	Net Chg.
PerDia	100	3 1/16	3 3/16	...
PtHel vtg .06e	61	17	17 1/2	
PtHel nv .06e	100	16	16 1/2	
Phrmtc	503	2	2	
Phrminc	65	2 1/4	2 19/...	
PhnxAd	621	7/32		
PhotScl 1.10	165	2 15/16		
PicktSu .90e	53	26	6 1/4	
Pikevle	13	37	4	
PinclFn	22	37	26 3/4	2
PloFn pf 1.88	4	2 7/16		
Players	106	3 1/16		
PlrMol	406	3/4		
Polydex	105	3 1/2		
Polymrx	391	13/−		
Powrec	160	4		
PwSpec	387			
PrabRbt	102			
Prstk un				
PrvB pf	.32			
PrvB un				
PrtHlt				
PrftTc				
Ps...				

The Wall Street Journal has a third OTC category for stocks that have very few issues changing hands. These are listed under "Additional NASDAQ Quotes." Only the bid and asked prices are given for these issues.

Other Markets

You may own a stock that is listed on the NYSE or AMEX and yet your broker may sell it for you on one of the regional exchanges in another city. Trades of stocks listed on both the NYSE and the regional exchanges are published in *The Wall Street Journal* under the heading "New York Stock Exchange Composite Trading." If a small company is only listed on a regional exchange but is actively traded, it will be listed under "U.S. Regional Markets." Stocks traded on the AMEX are listed under "American Stock Exchange Composite Trading."

The electronic ticker tape.

How to Understand the Ticker Tape

When the New York Mets won the World Series in 1986, New Yorkers went wild and honored the team with a "ticker tape" parade up Broadway. But there was no ticker tape. The paper that showered the players was confetti, not shredded ticker tape paper. That was not always the case. In 1927 Charles A. Lindbergh's parade, celebrating his solo flight across the Atlantic, was rained on by hundreds of thousands of pounds of shredded ticker tape paper that had been saved for the occasion. The paper came from the ticker machine, once the stockbroker's bible, but now an obsolete museum piece.

The Stock Ticker was invented by E.A. Calahan in 1867. Along with an earlier invention, the telegraph, it revolutionized Wall Street, sending trading prices around the country and popularizing the stock market with thousands of Americans. Thomas A. Edison improved Calahan's machine to such a degree that some models were called the Edison. By 1930 the ticker could print several hundred prices per minute by punching holes in the paper. As the tape moved along, it made a ticking sound, which is why it was called the ticker tape.

The electronic age has replaced the inch-wide tape with a computerized band that races across TV screens and desktop quote machines, carrying up-to-the-minute stock prices. The tape goes from the exchange floor to brokerage firms and the financial community. Cable TV networks can reproduce the ticker tape after a fifteen-minute delay.

The tape has two rows of information, one on top of the other. The top row has stock symbols, letters designating the name of the company, such as "GE" for General Electric, "DJ" for Dow Jones, "CLX" for Clorox Co. (Symbols for listed stocks are given in *Standard and Poor's Stock Guide*, available at brokerage firms and libraries.)

The bottom row shows the price per share and the number of shares traded in each transaction. Only the latest transaction is shown because the tape is continuously updated while the market is open. If just a price appears, then 100 shares have been traded. The small letter "s" and a number preceding the stock symbol indicate that a multiple of 100 shares were traded. For example, 25s40 1/2 means 2,500 shares were traded at 40 1/2. If the number before the "s" is above 10,000, then do not multiply it by 100; it already represents the actual total number of shares traded. For example, 200,000s46 1/2 means 200,000 shares traded at 46 1/2. A trade over 10,000 shares is a block trade.

There are no dollar signs on the tape. Occasionally letters follow the symbol, such as "PR," which indicates the transaction was for the company's preferred stock.

Since 1975, the NYSE and the AMEX have included in their separate tapes a symbol system to indicate when their stocks have traded on regional exchanges. The symbol follows an "&" and a dot after the stock symbol. For example, IBM&.P means trade took place on the Pacific Exchange.

The symbols used are as follows:
M = Midwest
X = Philadelphia
A = American
B = Boston
O = Other
N = New York
T = Third market
P = Pacific

SOME POPULAR STOCK SYMBOLS

AAPL	Apple Computer	HSY	Hershey Foods
C	Chrysler	IBM	International Business
F	Ford Motor		Machines
GEB	Gerber Products	KO	Coca-Cola
GM	General Motors	MCD	McDonald's
GS	Gillette	MOB	Mobil Oil

Note: *Apple Computer has four, not three letters in its symbol, indicating that it trades over-the-counter. The letter "Q" indicates a company is in bankruptcy.*

The Third Market is where non-exchange members and institutional investors trade exchange-listed securities in over-the-counter transactions.

Using Indexes and Averages

Because the stock market affects many aspects of our lives, nearly everyone, whether they own stocks or not, wants to know "what did the market do today?" Did it go up or down? Did it reach a new high or low? Now that you own Reebok stock, you too will want to keep up to date about the market.

Knowing how to interpret the stock tables enables you to keep track of individual stocks. Yet very often a stock behaves quite differently from other stocks or from the market as a whole.

In order to study the entire market or the big picture, you can follow the market indexes and averages. The two most widely used are the *Dow Jones Industrial Average*® and the *Standard & Poor's 500 Index*. These and other measurements track long-term trends, the ups and downs of the whole market over many years. They can alert you if your stock is ahead or behind the rest of the market so that you can then decide to sell or buy more shares.

STOCKS IN THE *DOW JONES INDUSTRIAL AVERAGE*®

Allied Signal	Boeing
Exxon	International Paper
Philip Morris	USX
Alcoa	Chevron
General Electric	McDonald's
Primerica	Union Carbide
American Express	Coca-Cola
General Motors	Merck
Procter & Gamble	United Technology
American Telephone	DuPont
& Telegraph	Minnesota Mining
Goodyear	& Manufacturing
Sears Roebuck	Westinghouse
Bethlehem Steel	Eastman Kodak
IBM	Navistar
Texaco	Woolworth

The oldest and most widely accepted indicator of the stock market's movement is the *Dow Jones Industrial Average*®. When the evening news commentator says, "The market went up 8 points today," he means the *Dow Jones Industrial Average*® rose 8 points over the day before. The Dow, sometimes called the DJIA, is expressed in points, not in dollars and cents because companies, prices, and adjustments of splits have changed so much since its inception.

The Dow is based on the stock prices of thirty leading companies which are representative of the largest industrial companies in the United States. It is determined by adding up the prices of all thirty stocks on the New York Stock Exchange on any one business day and then dividing by a special divisor which must be changed when one of the companies declares a stock split or markets additional shares. The divisors used for each of the averages are listed in the small print below the Dow charts in *The Wall Street Journal.*

There are two other Dow Jones Averages: the Transportation Average is made up of twenty airline, trucking, and railroad companies; the Utility Average includes fifteen gas and electric power companies; and the Dow Jones Composite consists of all sixty-five stocks.

The Dow and other averages measure the market's position at one time versus its past performance. The numbers represent changes in the value of billions of dollars in stock prices.

The Dow has been around since 1884, when Charles Dow drew up a list of the average closing prices of eleven stocks for his "Customer's Afternoon Letter." Nine were railroad stocks and the other two were business firms. Dow and his partner, Eddie Jones, founded the Dow Jones Company, a financial service firm, and they started *The Wall*

Street Journal. Today, the editors of *The Wall Street Journal* still decide which stocks in the Dow should be dropped and which ones will replace them.

• ***Other Indicators.*** The Dow is often criticized because a high-priced stock, such as IBM, has a greater influence on the market than a lower-priced one, such as Navistar. Other critics maintain its coverage is too narrow, since it is based on just thirty industrial and service industry stocks listed on the NYSE. Due in part to these shortcomings, other stock-market indicators, reflecting a broader aspect of the market, have come into existence. The best known is the *Standard & Poor's 500 Index*, or the S&P 500, as most people call it. Published by a financial service organization in New York, the S&P 500 was first introduced in the 1950s and is based on the performances of five hundred stocks. Most are traded on the NYSE, but some trade on the AMEX and OTC. Because some stocks have a greater influence on the market than others, the S&P 500 is "weighted," that is, in calculating the figure, the price of each stock is multiplied by the number of its common shares outstanding.

Other indicators you may see reference to are the *NYSE Composite*, which comprises all the stocks traded on the exchange; the *AMEX Market Value Index*, which covers the movement of about eight hundred stocks on the American Stock Exchange, and the *NASDAQ OTC Index,* which includes several thousand over-the-counter stocks. The broadest of all the indicators is the *Wilshire 5000 Equity Index.* Published in Santa Monica, California, the Wilshire measures the performance of all the NYSE and AMEX issues plus many OTC stocks. The *S&P OTC 250*, which covers over-the-counter stocks not listed on the exchanges, is another important broad indicator.

Why Does the Market Move?

There are a lot of factors that influence the movement of the market. The following are the most important:

> •interest rates
> •value of the dollar overseas
> •employment rates
> •tax rates
> •factory productivity
> •international conflicts
> •foreign stock markets
> •domestic political turmoil

Because these factors are continually changing, the market moves in cycles rather than in a straight line up or down. It tends to move up for a while and then reverses itself and drops for a period. The rising periods tend to take longer than the declines, rather like walking up a hill—it takes longer to get to the top than it does to get to the bottom.

When a market rises, it is called a *bull market*, and one who is optimistic about the market is called a *bull*. A *bear market* is a market in decline; a *bear* is one who is pessimistic about the market.

SEVEN SIGNS OF A COMING BEAR MARKET

- Fewer stocks hitting new highs each time the market hits a new high.
- Trading volume is decreasing on days when stock prices are increasing *and* increasing when prices are decreasing.
- Yields on money market funds are rising.
- Inflation (cost of living) is picking up.
- Interest rates on U.S. Treasury bills and bonds are rising.
- Stock prices are up 50 percent from their last cyclical low.
- Stocks move way up from historic P/E range.

THE ORIGINAL DOW STOCKS

Chicago & North Western	New York Central
Northern Pacific	Louisville & Nashville
Delaware, Lackawanna & Western	St. Paul
Union Pacific	Pacific Mail
Lake Shore Line	Western Union
Missouri Pacific	

There are several popular theories about the origin of the terms bull and bear. The most popular is that bears attack their enemy by patting their paws in a downward motion, while bulls, on the other hand, toss their horns upward before going after their prey.

One of the greatest bears of all time was Jacob Little, who capitalized on the famous Panic of 1837 in which banks failed and stock prices fell as people dumped their shares. Little made and lost four great fortunes through his bearish positions.

Up until Little's appearance, brokers were inevitably part-timers, trading securities only during the few short hours the exchange was open. Little, on the other hand, devoted all of his time to the market. Despite his dedication to the business, apparently he was widely disliked—he was blackballed several times before finally being accepted as a member of the NYSE.

Little wasn't always a winner. In the 1850s he lost a whopping $10 million in Erie stock in one day. Undaunted, the Great Bear stayed on Wall Street until the very end, trying to raise money for future speculations. According to Street mythology, his final words were: "I am going up. Who will go with me?"

Jacob Little, one of the great "bearish" investors, once lost $10 million in one day.

The Market News on Radio and TV

If you listen to the financial news for thirty minutes every other day, you will soon have a greater understanding of the market than most Americans. The key to smart investing is being up to date, and the media can help.

Select a radio or TV program that is accurate— and then, sift through the presentation carefully, sorting out fact from opinion, intelligent analysis from flamboyant personal statements. Avoid shows that are obvious commercials for a product, the speaker's or host's seminars, or an author's book.

And remember, any investing tips or stock ideas you hear on TV or radio are also heard by thousands of others. It's no longer a hot new idea.

TIPS FOR LISTENING TO THE NEWS

•Try to separate investment information from newsworthy filler.
•At the end of the show, ask yourself what you have learned. Stick with informative broadcasts.
•Keep a list of what you have learned in your financial notebook.
•Write down the names of stocks and who recommended them; put a star next to the winners.
•Keep a list of market forecasters and check back every three months to see whose forecasts were accurate.
•Don't feel you have to buy every stock that is recommended. The pros have a quip: "Sell on the news," which often applies to a recommendation made on a national broadcast.

THE TWO GREAT STOCK MARKET CRASHES

The market is a great place to be when the bull is roaring ahead, but when stocks come tumbling down and the bull retreats to his pen, it's devastating to everyone, not just those who own stock.

The two great financial disasters of this century were the Great Crash of 1929 and the more recent 1987 Crash, or "Black Monday." In ways they were alike, although the overall effects of the 1929 debacle were far more severe and widespread. In fact, the soaring hopes of the fabulous twenties vanished overnight as the Crash led immediately to the worst economic collapse in the history of America. The results of the '87 crash were neither as harsh nor as lasting.

In early 1929, millions of Americans were convinced they were riding on an escalator of financial progress. The wealthy and not-so-wealthy expressed their faith in the nation's economy by investing in the market. Stories of peddlers and middle-class workers who made fortunes overnight were rampant, and investors pushed up prices on the NYSE to heights that bore no resemblance to the actual growth of companies. By September 1929, stock prices were 400 percent above their levels of five years before. The bubble started to burst on October 23, when the market fell 31 points. On October 28, it fell another 49 points, and on the 29th, all the paper profits of the year were lost. Brokers and investors saw their empires crumble overnight. Some even jumped out of their office windows.

The collapse triggered the Great Depression, and America entered one of the most difficult decades of its history. The burdens of the Depression hurt nearly everyone, but weighed most heavily on the poor. Millions had no work, no food, and no housing. It took President Roosevelt's New Deal to turn the country around.

The next major crash also occurred in October; this time on the 19th, in 1987. On that day, the *Dow Jones Industrial Average*® fell an incredible 508 points, the largest one-day loss in its history. The blame was laid on program, or computerized, trading of large groups of stocks by professionals. And indeed, a cascade of sell orders from large institutions clogged the system and left many individual investors stranded while prices fell. The Presidential Task Force on Market Mechanisms, which studied the events leading up to October 19th, said that "small investors were at a disadvantage in speed of order execution" on Black Monday because the small order system, originally designed for the small investor, had been expanded to accomodate larger blocks of shares. And the buyers of last re-

After the 1929 crash: bargains everywhere.

sort, the specialists, were overwhelmed by sell orders and lacked the capital to support stock prices.

As in 1929, the chain of events leading up to the crash started far before that day. Many point to the day when news of a proposed tax change to make corporate takeovers less attractive was released. The prospect of more takeovers had helped prop up the market. Other factors cited as causing the October sell-off were high interest rates, inflated stock prices, and new statistics on the huge trade and budget deficits. There was no one clear-cut reason, but each of these factors built upon one another until a chain reaction was set in motion. Investors from the Far East to London to New York, linked by computers, frenetically leaped into selling. The next day, the Exchange came close to closing down.

Both stock market crashes serve to remind even the most optimistic investor that the old saying, "what goes up must come down," is indeed correct.

At a post display unit on the floor of the New York Stock Exchange, a trader tracks a stock's progress.

6

HOW TO BE A WALL STREET SLEUTH

B y now you realize there are thousands of stocks to buy, listed on one of the exchanges or over the counter. Selecting the right one for your portfolio may seem overwhelming but if at first you follow these three rules, you'll find it's like putting together the pieces of a puzzle. After you gain experience, you will develop your own methods for selecting stocks.

Rule 1. Buy stock in a company you already know something about. If you like using a particular computer, have a favorite cereal, or have fallen in love with a new camera, find out whether the company sells shares to the public. Among the areas to consider are the following:

- Foods and beverages
- Fast-food chains
- Restaurants
- Hotels and motels
- Banks
- Clothing

- Retail stores
- Entertainment
- Publishing
- Drugs and cosmetics
- Electronics
- Sporting goods

These categories, in which companies are grouped by their product or activity, are known on Wall Street as industries. Some industries are successful almost all the time, even when the economy is slowing down. They are called **recession resistant.** We all need to eat and take medicine, for example, even when we have less money than usual to spend. Therefore, food and drug stocks are called recession resistant. Other important recession-resistant groups are the utilities— gas, water, electric, and telephone companies.

Recession resistant: Stocks that tend to hold their price even during economically troubled times.

Rule 2. Investigate stocks of local companies. Find out what companies in your town or city are traded publicly. You can do this by calling a local stockbroker, asking someone you know who invests in stocks, or checking the list in your newspaper.

Rule 3. Consider buying stock in your local utility company. Many well-run utilities are safe and pay high dividends.

Gathering Research

Next, make a list of four or five possible stocks to buy, either stocks whose products you admire or those of familiar local companies. Then begin tracking down information on each one.

Step 1. Write or call the investor or shareholder relations office of each company on your list and ask for the annual and quarterly reports.

Step 2. Go to the library or a broker's office and check each company's write-up in *Value Line Investment Survey.* This research tool, which analyzes more than 1,700 companies, is updated weekly. It describes the company's business, products and services, financial health, and future prospects. Look at the top of each write-up for the safety and timeliness rankings. *Value Line* assigns each stock a number between 1 and 5 for these two rankings. A number 1 is given to companies that are the safest to buy, while a stock ranked 5 is considered to be a risky investment. A number 1 for timeliness means this is a good time to purchase shares, while a 5 signals caution.

Step 3. Call your broker and ask for the firm's research on these same companies.

Step 4. Take a close look at the annual report. (See below for how to read an annual report.) What is the earnings trend? What do you think of management? Does the company pay a dividend? Is the dividend rising?

Step 5. Follow the stock's price in the newspaper. If you buy, try to buy on a *dip,* that is, when the price is down slightly from its 52-week high.

Step 6. If you buy, write down in your financial notebook the reason you decided to invest in that company. You will refer back to this when you re-evaluate your stock later.

"Dear Shareholder" or: How to Read an Annual Report

Curling up with an annual report is a great way to check out a company's financial strength and learn the nitty-gritty of business finance. By understanding the contents of an annual report, you will master the basic building blocks of a business.

The annual report, written after the end of a corporation's **fiscal,** or business, year is its financial review issued to shareholders. If you are not a shareholder, you can get a copy of the annual

Fiscal: An accounting year consisting of twelve consecutive months, at the end of which a company's books are closed and the profit or loss for the year is determined. A company's fiscal year is often but not always the same as the calendar year. Seasonal businesses often elect a fiscal year so that the books are closed when there is the least inventory to handle.

report, free of charge, by calling the shareholder relations division of the company.

Here are the key elements found in all annual reports (They may appear in a slightly different order or the wording of the headings may vary.)

• ***The President's Letter.*** The report typically begins with a letter to shareholders from the president. It outlines important events of the past year and describes the current status of the company. Read with a dash of skepticism. Many letters are disguised public relations efforts, written with glowing optimism, with bad news downplayed.

• ***The Body.*** The main section covers the company's plans for the future, new products, information about the directors, and general comments on how each division has done during the year. Don't let glossy paper, artistic photos, and colorful graphics impress you. A simple presentation of the facts and a clear statement of financial statistics is what counts.

An annual report gives data on the financial health of a corporation to its stockholders.

The contents of the financial section are determined by Securities and Exchange Commission regulations. It must include the Balance Sheet, Income Statement, Source and Application of Funds, and the Auditor's Report.

• ***The Balance Sheet.*** This summary of assets and **liabilities** gives a quick snapshot of the financial condition of the company on the last day of the fiscal year. It also compares data from the end of the current fiscal year with data from the end of the last fiscal year. It is indeed a "balance" sheet, with assets on one side and liabilities on the other side. The difference between these two is what the stockholders own, or the **net worth** of the company. At all times, these three must be in balance:

Liabilities: Anything a person, company, or group owes; also called debt.

Net worth: The amount by which assets exceed liabilities.

$$Assets - Liabilities = Net\ Worth$$

The items in the assets column of the balance sheet are as follows:

1. Current assets consist of cash or cash equivalents and inventories of goods.

2. Fixed assets include machinery, factories, buildings, and other real estate.

Listed opposite the assets on the balance sheet are the liabilities. These include:

1. Current liabilities, or monies that are payable immediately or in the near future, such as unpaid wages, taxes due, or expenses payable.

2. Long-term liabilities, debts such as bonds or mortgages due to be paid off in anywhere from five to twenty years, or possibly longer.

You can determine whether a company is carrying too much long-term debt by dividing long-term debt by **total capital.** If it is below 50 percent, the company is probably financially sound. Obviously, the more debt a company has, the less financial cushion is available for weathering bad times.

Total capital: A company's long-term debt plus its equity.

- *Stockholders' Equity.* This is the value of all the assets owned by the company minus its liabilities. Stockholders' equity includes the value of the preferred and common stock, the money made from sale of the stock, and the profits that have been reinvested, which are called retained earnings. Stockholders' equity is sometimes referred to as the company's net worth. Net worth is not readily seen, like a pile of money in the bank; it is more amorphous in that it is the value of the shareholders' investment in the company.

- *Statement of Income and Retained Earnings.* This section shows the company's financial performance over a period of time. (The balance sheet, you recall, shows the firm's financial situation at a single moment in time.) The income statement adds up all the sales or revenues and then subtracts cost of goods sold and the expenses for selling these goods as well as operating the business. After dividends are paid to shareholders, the company has retained earnings to reinvest in expanding the company's business.

- *Statement of Changes in Financial Position,* also known as *Sources & Application of Funds Statement.* This portion of the report focuses on the company's working capital—that is, the money it uses to run the business on a day-to-day basis. It illustrates how much money or working capital was available and how the company used it.

- *Financial Summary, or Selected Highlights.* This table quickly shows the company's financial history over several years, including such key information as revenues, net income, earnings per share, and dividends. It may be at the front or the rear of the annual report. It shows whether earnings have been growing over the years.

• *Accountant's or Auditor's Report.* An independent accounting firm—that is, one not affiliated with the company—reviews all the data and verifies that the facts are true and that the company met the accounting principles required for public companies. If the corporation is having any problems, they will be mentioned here, often under the subheading "Qualification."

• *Footnotes.* The footnotes can be the most important part of an annual report. They tell whether there are any lawsuits or pending liabilities that could affect the company's financial future.

Analyzing a Company Like a Pro

Stock analysts use various ratios and figures to measure a company's value and performance. They are most meaningful when compared to past results and to other companies within the same industry or line of business.

• *Earnings Per Share.* This is one of the most often-used figures in analyzing a company and its stock because it usually has the greatest impact on a stock's price. To determine EPS, divide net earnings (listed in the income statement) by the number of shares outstanding. Because the number of shares outstanding can change—a company may issue more stock or buy some back—use the average number for the last day of the year as given in the annual report. Then compare EPS from one year to the next. A drop in EPS could signal problems; a steadily rising figure is a very healthy sign. As a rule of thumb, an annual increase of at least 10 percent in EPS indicates sound growth.

• *Price/Earnings Ratio.* A stock's market price divided by its earnings per share. A low P/E usually signals a stable, mature company, while a

high P/E indicates that rapid growth is expected. A
high P/E may also indicate that a stock is over-
priced.

• *Dividend Yield.* Dividend per share divided
by stock price. Use to compare income from
different stocks. A high-yielding stock is more
attractive to investors seeking immediate income
rather than a long-term investment.

• *Dividend Payout.* Dividend per share divided
by earnings per share. This tells what percentage of
earnings is paid out in dividends.

• *Book Value.* Shareholders' equity (assets
minus liabilities) divided by the number of shares
outstanding. This is what each shareholder would
get if the company were liquidated. Book value is
sometimes understated because companies include
assets at their cost price rather than their current
sale value. Land and other real estate is frequently
listed below sale value.

Key Questions the Annual Report Will Answer

• *Is the company solvent?* Divide total current
assets by total current liabilities. A ratio of two to
one is generally considered good. A decreasing
ratio over the years may spell trouble.

• *Is the company profitable?* Divide net profit
by sales. This indicates the profit earned for each
dollar of sales. It shows whether the company is
efficient.

• *Can the company pay its immediate debts?*
Divide cash plus accounts receivable by total
current liabilities. The result is the amount in liquid
assets available to meet current debt. If the ratio is
one to one or more, the company is regarded as
liquid. The higher the ratio, the more liquid the
company.

The 10-K Report

Even more details about a company are given in a 10-K report, also filed annually with the SEC. Although they are not usually mailed out to investors, you can get one free from any company. (10-K refers to the number of the SEC form used.)

The 10-K details the company's lines of business, all products, and facilities. It tells of plant or store closings, sales of property, the competition the company faces, relevant government regulations, environmental problems, and troublesome legal proceedings.

Setting Your Investment Goals: Growth vs. Income

As you study various companies, you should be thinking about your investment goals and your tolerance for risk. Do you want to make your capital grow to meet a future goal, such as paying for part of your college expenses, or do you want income you can spend now? One of the biggest mistakes many investors make is not determining why they are buying a stock before they do so. Having a clear goal in mind helps you pick the best stocks.

There are two basic investment objectives: income and capital appreciation. *Income* refers to the amount a stock (or any investment) will pay on a regular basis. With stocks, income is paid in the form of a dividend based on the company's earnings and profits. *Capital appreciation* refers to how much the original investment, or *principal,* grows in price. Growth stocks traditionally offer higher rates of capital appreciation than income stocks. But the gain is not realized until the stock is sold at a higher price than the investor originally paid for it. With income stocks, on the other hand, shareholders receive regular dividend income checks. The two types of stocks are not mutually exclusive. Sometimes income stocks go up in price and some growth stocks pay dividends. Your portfolio can consist of both types; just don't expect a growth stock to pay a high dividend, or an income stock to shoot up in price.

Diversification

As you build your portfolio, be certain to diversify—*never* put all your eggs in one basket. By purchasing stocks of several companies in various industries, you spread out your risk and protect yourself against an unfortunate turn of events in any one company or industry. Ultimately you should own eight to ten—enough for adequate diversification but not too many to manage. Your portfolio should include some **blue chips**, some stocks for income, and some for growth.

Types of Stocks

Income Stocks

Income stocks pay a high current yield and usually are above average in safety. They include electric utility companies, telephone companies, oil stocks, **closed-end bond fund** stocks, real estate investment trusts stocks (called **REITs**), and some blue-chip stocks.

For names of top-yielding stocks, check the list under the headings "High-Yielding Stocks" and "High-Yielding Non-Utility Stocks" in the current index of *Value Line Investment Survey.*

Defensive Stocks

Defensive stocks are issues of large, financially solid companies that have maintained a dominant position in their industry for many years. Defensive stocks have long histories of earnings growth and

Blue-chip stocks: High-quality stocks with a long history of sustained earnings and dividends. The phrase comes from poker, in which the blue chip is the most expensive and valuable token in the game.

Closed-end bond fund: An investment company that operates like a mutual fund but has a limited number of shares outstanding. Shares trade on an exchange.

REIT: Publicly traded company that manages real estate to make money for shareholders. Some REITs lend money to developers, others own actual property.

DIFFERENT TYPES OF STOCKS

BLUE-CHIP STOCKS	GROWTH STOCKS
IBM	COMPAQ Computer
General Electric	Safety Kleen
Coca-Cola	Waste Management
INCOME STOCKS	CYCLICAL STOCKS
AT&T	Reynolds Metals
NYNEX	Ford Motor
Iowa-Illinois Gas & Electric	Inland Steel
DEFENSIVE STOCKS	SPECULATIVE STOCKS
Pepsi-Cola	LoneStar Industries
Campbell Soup	Santa Fe Pacific
Hershey Foods	Long Island Lighting

dividend payouts. However, their dividends are usually not as high as those of income stocks. Look for the list "Conservative Stocks" in the *Value Line Investment Survey's* index.

Growth Stocks

Growth stocks are issues of companies expected to grow faster than the overall economy. Dividends are typically below average, since they generally plow a large portion of earnings back into the company to finance research, development, and expansion. However, their stock prices tend to move up more rapidly than prices of other types of stocks.

The index of *Value Line* Index lists these stocks under these headings: "High Growth Stocks" and "Lowest P/E Stocks."

Cyclical Stocks

Cyclical stocks are issues of companies in industries affected by both business cycles and consumer demand. When the overall economy is booming and demand is up, these stocks tend to move up in price. During recessionary cycles, these stocks usually perform poorly. In order to invest wisely in this area, study **economic forecasts**, such as employment trends and the cost of food and oil and how busy the nation's factories are.

Economic forecasts: Studies that compile and analyze current statistics in order to find trends and help predict the future of the economy. Among the areas of focus: housing starts, automobile sales, and interest rates.

Speculative Stocks

Speculative stocks carry a higher degree of risk because they are issues of unknown or new companies. Sometimes established companies that have fallen on hard times but are about to turn around are also found in the speculative category. These stocks may be able to achieve more rapid growth than larger companies, but they also tend to react sharply to changes in the economy and lag behind a strong bull market as investors flock to more popular issues.

How Much Risk?

As your portfolio grows in size, think about the amount of risk you wish to take. You should not take more risk than you can afford. There is a direct connection between risk and reward, called the risk/reward ratio. Simply stated, the greater the expected return, the greater the risk. A savings account in a bank is a very safe investment. But there is no possibility for growth beyond the interest being earned, so this investment has low risk/low expected return. On the other hand, stock in a new company is an unknown but if its product is successful the stock's price could double or even triple. Or you could lose your entire investment. This is a high risk/high reward investment.

J. PIERPONT MORGAN

J. Pierpont Morgan was a broker and investment banker who began as an accountant in his father's banking firm and ended up controlling the New York Central Railroad in 1879 at the age of 42. He was a powerful man accustomed to dominating every situation, and it was said that stock prices rose and fell based on Morgan's decision whether or not to be on a company's board of directors.

In 1901 Morgan astonished Wall Street by arranging and financing the merger which gave birth to the nation's first billion dollar company, the U.S. Steel Corporation. He bought some of John D. Rockefeller's iron mines and all of Andrew Carnegie's steel business. It was the most expensive consolidation in U.S. history. After the deal went through, Morgan reportedly told a journalist who asked him if he was going to live abroad, as was rumored: "America's good enough for me." William Jennings Bryan, the great lawyer and politician, said in response: "Whenever he doesn't like it, he can give it back!"

In March 1907, a wave of panic hit Wall Street. Many of the big investors unloaded $800 million in securities within a short period of time. The leading stocks plummeted in price and bank runs became almost daily events. One large bank, Knickerbocker Trust Co., was forced to close its doors and the panic began to spread to banks all over the nation.

Morgan stepped in and pressured the leading bankers of New York to join forces to prevent a total financial collapse of the country. A single banking trust, he said, would be created, with every institution represented in the room contributing to the giant trust. Morgan's own group, of course, would have controlling interest. The presidents of the banks, each powerful men in their own right, were given no choice, but just in case they thought about leaving without signing the agreement, Morgan had locked the door of his library and put the key in his waistcoat pocket.

When news of the meeting reached the public the next day, stock prices immediately went up and the banking crisis of 1907 was averted. When someone criticized Morgan for exerting such total control over the nation's finances, he said: "I'm not in Wall Street for my health."

Morgan died six years later, leaving behind not only a financial fortune but also a large art collection, much of it housed today in the Morgan Library in New York.

J. P. Morgan

Many investors now choose to invest by personal computer.

WINNING ON WALL STREET

I n this chapter we will describe the various
ways to boost your portfolio power. You
may not be able to use each one right now,
but in the future one or more of these ways
to manage your money will be helpful. Finally, you
will learn the basics of market timing—when to buy
and when to sell stocks.

There is much folklore about the best time to
buy stocks, such as the day before a major holiday,
just after a presidential election, or when the length
of women's hemlines rises. Supposedly, when
hemlines move up, the market will rise, and when
hemlines drop, the market soon follows. While
these theories are amusing, you should not take
them too seriously. Let the length of women's skirts
remain a fashion concept, not a technique for
selecting stocks.

Mark Twain understood better than most the foolishness of relying on such theories as the time of the year for "speculating" in the market:

"October. This is one of the most peculiarly dangerous months to speculate in stocks. The others are July, January, September, April, November, May, March, June, December, August, and February." (*Pudd'nhead Wilson*)

WALL STREET FOLKLORE

Some people believe that certain days are better for buying stock than others. The American Association of Independent Investors has noticed the following trends:

•Stock prices usually fall on Mondays but rise on Tuesdays through Fridays.

• On all days, prices level off until the last fifteen minutes of trading when they start to rise.

•Stocks have their largest price increase on the last day of trading for each month and on the first three days of the next month.

•Prices rise before holidays.

•The market's favorite holidays, in order of preference, are:

> Labor Day
> Memorial Day
> Thanksgiving
> New Year's Day
> Christmas
> Good Friday
> Fourth of July

Finding Money to Invest

In order to build your portfolio, you must come up with some cash. Perhaps you already have a small amount in your savings account. If not, take a look at the list of possible sources of money below. Then add your own ideas.

• Earnings from a summer or after school job
• Allowance. Save a percentage, say 25 percent,

on a regular basis, and put it in a savings account where it will earn interest until you have enough to purchase a stock.
- Birthday and holiday gifts
- Graduation gifts

Investing by Computer

The stock market crash of 1987 impressed upon many investors the importance of being able to place buy and sell orders quickly and of keeping up to date with what's happening on Wall Street—difficult to do if your broker's telephone is constantly busy. Investing by personal computer ("on-line trading") is one way around this problem.

The largest provider of desktop investing services is San Francisco-based Charles Schwab & Co., the discount broker, with its Equalizer program. Fidelity Investment Co., the Boston-based mutual fund company, and other discount brokerage firms, such as New York's Quick & Reilly with Quick Way, and major banks with investing divisions, offer similar services.

Full-service brokerage firms do not provide on-line trading to their customers. Their computerized systems deliver information to their brokers, who in turn sell investments to their clients.

How It Works

It's simple. Virtually anyone with a personal computer (a PC) and a **modem** can get access to on-line services. You need to purchase a software program—a set of instructions that allows a PC to get on-line service and to send and receive information. Once this equipment is in place, you simply dial a certain telephone number, enter an identification number and/or password, and you are connected with a host computer, which is usually a public

Modem: A device that hooks up to a personal computer, making it possible to communicate between computers over the telephone.

database. The host computer then accesses the brokerage house, although with some systems you are connected immediately with the brokerage firm's computer, bypassing the public database.

When your order reaches the brokerage house, it is usually reviewed quickly by a broker and then forwarded to the floor of the exchange or put into the electronic DOT system.

After the order is executed, the investor receives an electronic confirmation. Brokerage houses also send written confirmation through the mail.

Just the Facts, Ma'am

Most systems allow users to check current stock prices, place their orders, and review their portfolio status at no cost. For a fee, investors can get additional information to help analyze stocks.

Start-up costs vary, but are minimal for those who already own a PC and modem. Trading time (getting prices, placing orders, and checking portfolios) is usually free after paying a sign-up fee. In some cases, there's no sign-up fee. Instead, per-minute charges are imposed. With most systems, charges are significantly lower for nighttime use.

Public Data Bases

• *Dow Jones News/Retrieval.* This service is all-inclusive and expensive, but difficult for beginners to use. It provides historical and current information on companies, analysts' reports, news stories, and special features from *The Wall Street Journal* and *Barron's*. Up-to-the-minute news from the Dow Jones News Service can also be accessed. This late-breaking news is not offered by any other on-line service. The stories stay on-line for ninety days.

• *CompuServe.* This database is similar to the Dow Jones News/Retrieval, although it does not include the Dow Jones News/Retrieval news stories. Inves-

tors can search for stocks to buy through a database
of 90,000 securities that are traded in the United
States and Canada. For example, you can get the
names of all stocks on the NYSE priced under $30
per share that also pay dividends. Or you can get a
list of all stocks with a P/E ratio under 12—within a
few minutes.

ON-LINE SYSTEMS

Before You Go On-Line:
• Call several discount brokerage firms or a major bank and ask them
  to send you information about their on-line trading system.
• Then call several of the major database systems listed below for
  their material. Be certain to get price structures for each plan.
  CompuServe   800-848-8990 or 614-457-8600
  P.O. Box 20212
  Columbus, OH 43220

  Dow Jones News/Retrieval   800-522-3567 or 609-452-1511
  P.O. Box 300
  Princeton, NJ 08543

  The Equalizer   800-334-4455
  Schwab Investor Information
  101 Montgomery Street
  San Francisco, CA 94104

Investment Games

You may want to sharpen your investment skills by
using a computer game before tackling real-life
investments with real dollars. There are a handful
of such computerized market games being sold—
Baron (a real estate game), Millionaire (a stock-
market game), and Tycoon (a commodities game).
Team up with several other computer buffs and
share the bill. Most computerized finance games
are priced around $50.

Also, schools in many states across the country participate in *The Stock Market Game*™, sponsored by the Securities Industry Foundation for Economic Education. In a classroom setting, students learn about investing by creating a portfolio based on actual stocks and compete against teams from other schools. Awards are given to the teams whose portfolios show the greatest increase in market value at the end of a ten-week period. For more information, write to:

Securities Industry Foundation for Economic Education
    c/o Securities Industry Association
    120 Broadway, 35th Floor
    New York, NY 10271
    Tel: (212) 608-1500

The Chicago Board of Trade runs a similar game, called *Commodity Challenge*. Students participating in this game are judged on the soundness of the reasoning behind their investment choices.

Start Your Own Investment Club

One way to buy stocks that's fun and inexpensive is through an investment club made up of friends, relatives, or neighbors. By pooling your money with that of other club members, you can afford to purchase more stock than you could on your own. You also have interested people with whom to learn about the market, hash over ideas, and share successes and failures. Here's how to start one in your town.

The Seven Steps

   Step 1. Put a notice in your school newspaper, on the bulletin board at the local YMCA/HA or YWCA/HA, or at your church or synagogue, asking interested investors to contact you. Talk to family and friends. Try to interest about fifteen to twenty people in the club. If all members are under your state's legal age, ask an adult to be your sponsor.

Step 2. Before your first meeting, call or write the National Association of Investors Corp. (NAIC), 1515 East Eleven Mile Road, Royal Oak, MI 48067 (313-543-0612), a nonprofit educational organization. They will send you a free pamphlet entitled "Suggested Steps for Starting an Investment Club." Follow these steps carefully.

Step 3. Call your first meeting. Discuss the purpose of the club, the yearly dues, and the amount each member plans to invest. The average club in the United States has sixteen members, each contributing $35 per month. Once the club is officially formed, join the National Association of Investors Club. Membership is $30 a year for the group, with an additional $8 for each individual member. It is well worth the cost. You receive instructions on setting up and running a club, as well as excellent, easy-to-understand research on what stocks to buy.

Step 4. Elect officers. The key position is that of treasurer—this officer handles dues, monthly contributions, and stock trades. This person should be able to use a computer and keep track of these details. Elect another member to coordinate stock research assignments. Rotate research so that each person will learn how to analyze stocks.

Step 5. Select the day of each month that you will hold meetings, and be consistent. Although you can rotate the meeting place from house to house, the meeting day should be firm.

Step 6. Decide what stockbroker to use and what type of club to form—a partnership or a corporation are the usual choices. The NAIC will help with these and other details, such as filing for a federal tax identification number, which is required to open a brokerage account, keeping proper records for contributions and withdrawals, and registering stock certificates. If the club does its own research, it can probably save on commissions by using a discount broker. Compare rates with a full-service firm first—some actually have lower maximums on small transactions than discount firms have. A full-service firm may also give a local investment club a break on commissions. If the club uses a full-service broker, try not to rely on his or her advice too much. One purpose of a club is to learn about investing, and that means making your own decisions—even if a pro could do better.

Step 7. Determine a procedure for researching companies, deciding what to buy, how many shares to buy, and when to sell. In a typical club, one or two people present the results of companies they've researched at the monthly meeting. Then a vote is taken, with the majority deciding whether to buy or not. Club members, just like Wall Street pros, seldom make unanimous decisions about stocks.

The Team Way
During the first year, it is a good idea to have everyone contribute the same dollar amount. This can be adjusted later on, if the membership is in agreement. But keep increments to $10 units to simplify bookkeeping. To avoid one person taking over the club, set a top and a bottom monthly dollar contribution and specify that no one member can increase his or her capital contribution to more than 20 percent of the club's total investment fund. That eliminates having an in-house dictator.

Reducing Commissions
You can eliminate some brokerage commissions if the club invests in any of the companies that are part of the NAIC's Low-Cost Investment Plan.

Under this plan, clubs can buy as little as one share at the market price from well-known companies, such as McDonald's, Quaker Oats, Mobil Oil, and Walt Disney. There is a one-time charge of $5 per company. Most companies in this plan allow dividends to be reinvested in additional shares.

If you decide to start or join a club, make it a year-long commitment. Investment clubs are not suitable for short-term trading.

Reinvesting Dividends for Profits
Automatic Dividend Reinvestment Plans (DRIPs)

Once you have purchased your first shares, you will want to increase your portfolio. The simplest way is to reinvest your dividends instead of spending them. Automatic dividend reinvestment plans, sometimes referred to as DRIPs, are offered by more than 1,000 companies to their shareholders.

Under this plan, neither you nor your broker receive your dividend checks. Instead, you authorize the company to reinvest your dividends in additional shares of the same stock you already own. You increase your holdings and at the same time avoid a stockbroker's commissions. Some companies even offer a 3 to 5 percent discount on the market price of the new shares of stock. Other companies allow investors to make cash payments into their account to buy more shares. McDonald's, for example, permits cash contributions of up to $75,000 per year.

When you initially purchase any stock, ask the investor relations department if a DRIP plan is available. If it is, they will mail you an authorization form.

Write to the following source and request a free copy of their annual update on dividend reinvestment programs:

Investment clubs help students learn about the stock market.

Dow Theory Forecasts, Inc.
7412 Calumet Avenue
Hammond, Indiana 46324-2692

Before You Sign On

• Find out how many shares you need to enroll in the plan. With some companies, a single share is sufficient; others require 25, 50, or 100 shares.

• Ask whether there is a fee.

• Determine whether you can buy additional shares for cash.

• Scrutinize any company offering to reinvest your dividends at a discount. Check their earnings figures carefully. The offer could mean that the stock is floundering and the company has introduced a discount to attract buyers for its shares.

The Blueprint Program ™

If you have saved $100, you can begin investing in stocks through a special program for small investors. It makes buying that first stock a cinch.

Merrill Lynch is the only brokerage firm currently offering this mini-investor's plan. They call it The Blueprint Program™.

After your initial investment of at least $100, you can make investments in any dollar amount you like. There is no requirement for how often or how much you invest after your initial purchase. Because investments are made by the dollar amount and not by the number of shares of stock, you wind up purchasing fractional shares and diversifying your portfolio for very little money.

Dividends are automatically reinvested in the companies you've selected and commissions are low—up to 55 percent less than the regular rates. Lists of recommended stocks, for long-term investing, are mailed periodically to participants.

For a brochure and the current list of stocks suggested for purchase, contact:

> Merrill Lynch & Co.
> Blueprint Program™
> P.O. Box 30441
> New Brunswick, NJ 08989-0441
> Telephone: 800-637-3766

When and What to Buy

A company should have a number of characteristics and qualities in order for it to be worth adding to your portfolio. Everyone who invests has their own ideas about what is a good stock. However, some factors have proven to be successful over and over

How to Hold Down Losses

- Set an exact dollar amount (a stop-loss price) for selling shares of stocks you own.
- Give this information to your broker. Your stock will then be sold automatically if it drops to the stop-loss price.
- Most stop-loss prices are set from 10 percent to 25 percent below the current price.
- Adjust the stop-loss price upwards if the stock rises in price.

Caution: Stop orders are not foolproof. The stock may plunge below the sell price before your order can be executed. Or you may lose out on a big stock recovery. But in the long run, you will come out ahead.

in judging a stock's quality and future performance. Look for a company that has the following:

• *Strong management.* The best-managed companies make the most money in the long run. Management that owns substantial amounts of the company's stock has an added incentive to make the shares more valuable. New managers with successful track records at other companies may be able to turn around an ailing company.

• *Low debt level.* Current assets should be at least twice as high as current liabilities. You want a company that can pay its bills.

• *Low P/E ratios.* If the P/E ratio is lower than average for the industry (given in *Value Line*), or lower than the average for the market as measured by the *S&P 500's* P/E, the stock may be undervalued and will rise in price.

• *Smart marketing.* A company that promotes its product well generally attracts new customers and keeps sales levels high.

• *Significant market share.* A company that is a leader in its industry is likely to have lower production costs because the costs are spread out over the larger number of units produced. *Caution:* If production facilities are old and obsolete, the opposite is true.

• *Appropriate dividend payments.* A good growth company pays out less than 50 percent of its earnings in dividends. The opposite is true for an income stock.

• *Increasing earnings per share.* Earnings should grow at approximately the same rate as sales.

• *Assets below value.* A company whose assets per share are at or below their market price is often a *takeover candidate,* a company that other corporations are interested in buying.

WARNING SIGNS: WHEN TO SELL A STOCK

Since it's better to sell too early than too late, *consider selling* when you see the following warning signs:

- These fundamentals deteriorate:
  - profit margins
  - market share
  - earnings growth rate
  - unit growth rate
- The company reduces or cancels the dividend.
- The company has exceptionally high debt.
- The company receives unfavorable reports by several analysts.
- The company stock lags behind its industry group.
- An anticipated event never happens, such as a takeover offer, a merger, an invention, or a new product introduction.
- The P/E ratio rises rapidly.
- The price reaches your target price.

- *Strong cash flow.* A steady flow of cash means a company can meet its bills and have money left over to pay a high dividend or to reinvest in the company. These companies, too, are often takeover candidates.

When to Sell

The only successful rule in stock investing is: *Buy low and sell high.* Buying low is relatively easy, but letting go, whether a stock goes up or down, is understandably much more difficult. When the price falls, it's tempting to put off selling and hope for a recovery. On the other hand, when the price rises, greed may take over and one hopes for even greater profits!

Don't Fall in Love With Your Stock

If you cling to a stock that has not met your expectations, remember: It isn't what you make on paper that counts, it's what you keep.

• Review your initial reasons for buying the stock. (You wrote down this reason in your financial notebook.) Did you think a new product would be successful, for instance? If that hasn't happened, it may be time to sell. Don't bury your head in the sand: acknowledge an error and move on. You can't expect to hit home runs all the time.

• Anticipate selling when you buy. Pick a target price, both up and down, and sell when your stock reaches either point. The rule of thumb is to sell after a stock loses 10 percent in price.

• Continually ask yourself: Would I buy this stock today at this price? Think of all stocks as "buys" or "sells" and never merely as "holds."

• Factor into your decision the type of stock you own: *Cyclical stocks* perform well in their cycle; *growth stocks* can be held longer term; and *income stocks* are suitable as long as their dividends are sufficiently high.

• Begin to consider selling when a company's earnings are down from the previous year.

• Compare your stock with some relevant index, such as the Dow Jones or *S&P 500*. If your stock is doing better than the market, consider buying more shares. If it's doing worse, sell.

• Watch interest rates. Rising rates tend to hurt stocks by pulling investors' money away from the market and into certificates of deposit, savings accounts, and other investments paying higher rates. Track the direction of interest rates by checking the prime rate listed in the newspaper. The prime rate is the interest rate banks charge their most credit-worthy customers. When a leading bank reduces or raises its prime, other banks tend to follow.

Finally, remember that millionaires know when to get into the market, and when to get out.

JAMES FISK: A WALL STREET LEGEND

James Fisk was one of Wall Street's greatest speculators and manipulators. Although he ran his own firm, his most outlandish deals were done with a partner, Jay Gould. Gould, who was famous in his own right, was cold and serious whereas Fisk was raucous and fun-loving. Together they made a great team. Born in Pownal, Vermont, in 1834, Fisk worked for a circus as a child and waited on tables at his father's hotel, The Revere House, in Brattleboro, Vermont. The guests found the young Fisk charming and entertaining. So did Lucy Moore, whom he married when he was only nineteen. Although they were married for seventeen years, the longest period they lived together in the same house was six months. Yet they remained friends until Fisk's death.

Fisk had owned a brokerage firm, but his notoriety stems mostly from his flamboyant personality and his outlandish deals with his partner, Jay Gould. In addition to helping Gould engineer an attempt to corner the gold market (see page 63), Fisk joined Gould and another wheeler-dealer, Daniel Drew, in a wild battle to wrest control of the Erie Railroad from Cornelius Vanderbilt.

They used every means available to seize the railroad and at one point had to flee to New Jersey to avoid arrest by the sheriff of New York for stock manipulation. They waited out the long battle for the Erie Railroad as temporary refugees at Taylor's Hotel in Jersey City, which they turned into a garrison protected by large cannons. Gould and Fisk finally took over the Erie Railroad in 1868 with Gould as president and Fisk as controller.

Although Fisk was wise in the ways of business, he was unlucky in love. He was shot to death on the staircase of the Grand Central Hotel in New York by Edward S. Stokes, a former business associate and arch rival for the attention of a well-known actress, Josie Mansfield.

Although Fisk's escapades were legend, his estate was not. The great manipulator left less than a million dollars, most of it to Mrs. Fisk and apparently none to Josie. His possessions were auctioned off, including the beloved canaries he raised. One canary, named Jay Gould, fetched $8.50, while the bird named Cornelius Vanderbilt brought $6.50.

Cartoon of Fisk juggling his holdings, 1870

To be successful in the stock market you must be able to make decisions quickly.

WORKING IN THE STOCK MARKET

T he world of investing, whether it is on Wall Street in New York or on Main Street in your home town, is exciting, fast-paced, and competitive. If you are intrigued by the stock market and think you might like to make it your career, begin learning about it now.

Your Preliminary Investigation

1. Visit your school career office or the public library and gather the available material on the securities industry.

2. Call the office manager of a local brokerage firm or bank that has a brokerage subsidiary. Explain that you are considering a career in the securities business and you would like to visit their office to learn more about the field. Visit after the market closes, when stockbrokers are less busy.

THE FIRST WOMEN BROKERS

Two women shocked New York's Victorian society in 1869 by announcing their intention to open a Wall Street brokerage office. Victoria Claflin Woodhull and her sister, Tennessee Celeste Claflin, ardent feminists, began their operations from a parlor in the Fifth Avenue Hotel. Cornelius Vanderbilt, the wealthy New York magnate, was intrigued by the sisters, and backed them to the amount of $7,500. They used this money to open an office the following year at 44 Broad Street, in the heart of the business district. It's possible that Vanderbilt funded the "lady brokers," as they were called, because his wife was a feminist.

The presence of women in business on Wall Street was considered outrageous. In fact, almost one hundred years passed before the first woman held a seat in her own name on the New York Stock Exchange.

But the "lady brokers" were so popular with gawkers and tourists that a sign had to be hung: "ALL GENTLEMEN WILL PLEASE STATE THEIR BUSINESS AND THEN RETIRE AT ONCE."

Despite the fact that many men on Wall Street did not take the Claflin sisters seriously, their firm, Woodhull, Claflin & Co., was profitable within six months. After making a large splash and a modest success on Wall Street, the Claflin sisters soon closed shop and moved to England.

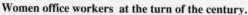

Women office workers at the turn of the century.

3. Contact a university that offers a Masters in Business (MBA) degree. The catalog will describe the necessary courses and give a general description of the program. Among the leading schools offering the MBA program are Columbia, Harvard, University of Pennsylvania, Northwestern, and Stanford.

4. Write to the sources at the end of this section to request additional career information.

The Necessary Skills

Although interest and determination are the key prerequisites for success in any job, certain skills are helpful in a Wall Street career. You must be able to make decisions under pressure and to work in a hectic environment. In addition, you should enjoy several of the following:

- Solving mathematical and statistical problems
- Number crunching: Doing ratios, formulas, and percentages
- Reading about business and economics
- Selling (for brokerage business)
- Doing research
- Writing reports

Suggested High School or College Courses

In order to be successful in this field, you need a well-rounded education and an interest in national and world events. Liberal arts courses are a sound basis for preparing for a Wall Street career. In addition, take as many of these courses as possible:

Algebra	Communications
Calculus	Economics
Marketing	Salesmanship
Accounting	Corporate finance
Mathematics	Business

All professional positions in the field require a Bachelor of Arts degree. Many firms also hire Masters in Business graduates, but this is not an entry-level requirement. In fact, the major investment banking firms and brokerage houses have extensive in-house training programs for those with a bachelors degree and will send promising young employees to school for their masters degree.

Types of Jobs

The three institutions where you are most likely to find a job are brokerage firms, investment banking houses, and commercial banks. The key positions are securities broker, floorbroker, specialist, securities analyst, portfolio manager, corporate finance analyst, and investment banker.

• *Securities broker.* Stockbrokers, also called registered representatives, account executives, or simply brokers, are the people who buy and sell stocks and other securities for clients and institutions. Brokers also offer investment advice and help investors reach their financial goals. Many help investors put together a total financial plan that includes a proper balance between savings, securities, real estate, and other investments. Brokers are employed by brokerage firms, investment banks, and mutual funds. They must pass the Series Seven exam given by the National Association of Security Dealers. This exam tests the candidate's basic knowledge about the stock market, margin accounts, dividends, stock splits, and many other points. For additional information, contact:

• *The Securities Training Corporation,* which gives the training and study sessions for all levels of securities exams: 17 Battery Place, New York, NY 10004.

- *The New York Institute of Finance,* which prepares students for a number of positions in the industry: 2 Broadway, New York, NY 10004.
- *The Securities Industry Association,* which is a trade group for brokerage firms that lobbies in Washington for its members' interests—before Congress and the SEC: 120 Broadway, 35th Floor, New York, NY 10271.
- *The National Association of Security Dealers,* if you are interested in an investigative position, examining the records of the brokerage houses to see that their operations are correctly run: 1735 K Street NW, Washington, D.C. 20006.

Early in the trading day at the New York Stock Exchange.

• ***Investment banking.*** Investment bankers offer three services to their clients: (1) they advise corporations on financial strategies (generally called corporate finance), (2) they help bring companies public (called underwriting), and (3) they distribute or sell large blocks of securities. Some investment banks specialize in mergers and acquisitions, helping companies plan the purchase or sale of another company or a subsidiary. To accomplish all of these activities, investment banks have large research departments.

Investment banks hire both MBAs and BAs, placing the latter in two-year training programs. BAs are generally expected to go on to graduate school. The hours are long and the pressure intense.

• ***Analysts.*** Large brokerage firms and investment banks hire research staff, called securities analysts, to provide reports on individual companies and to suggest whether or not to buy the company's stock. Most analysts follow several industries, the entertainment or fast-food industries, for example. These stock detectives must be able to spot trends before others. In order to gather information, they are in constant communication with the management of the companies they follow, often visiting their headquarters.

• ***Portfolio manager.*** This position involves selecting securities, deciding the correct balance between stocks and bonds, and working with securities analysts to determine which securities should be held and which sold. Portfolio managers oversee investments for large clients, which are usually institutions, but can also be for very wealthy individuals. They are hired by large institutions, such as mutual fund companies, by corporations with large pension funds for employees, or by companies that manage money for individual clients.

WOMEN ON WALL STREET

Woman pages, 1940s

Although the Claflin sisters may have been the first female brokers, women did not appear on the floor of the New York Stock Exchange until World War II, when men trooped off to serve their country. The women had to leave when the war ended and the men returned. The exchange remained a men's club for years, although in 1940 Muriel Audrey Bailey became a general partner of Belden & Co., a New York Stock Exchange member firm. Bailey paved the way for other women on Wall Street, although she was not a member of the exchange itself.

That particular barrier was broken by Muriel F. Siebert in the 1960s. She arrived in New York driving a second-hand Studebaker, with $500 in her pocket. Her first job on Wall Street was at Bache & Co., where she was paid $65 a week as a research trainee. She was assigned airline stocks because the firm's transportation analyst was more interested in

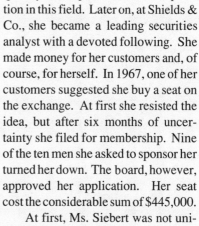

studying other companies. Siebert quickly developed an excellent reputation in this field. Later on, at Shields & Co., she became a leading securities analyst with a devoted following. She made money for her customers and, of course, for herself. In 1967, one of her customers suggested she buy a seat on the exchange. At first she resisted the idea, but after six months of uncertainty she filed for membership. Nine of the ten men she asked to sponsor her turned her down. The board, however, approved her application. Her seat cost the considerable sum of $445,000.

At first, Ms. Siebert was not universally welcomed on the floor, but eventually the presence of a female in what had been a male bastion since 1792 became acceptable.

In 1970, Jane R. Larkin became the second woman member. Today there are 69 women members and two women who sit on on the board of directors of the exchange.

Muriel F. Siebert

APPENDIX

Visiting a Stock Exchange

If you live near one of the exchanges, or you are taking a trip to one of these cities, make time to visit the stock exchange. Most have viewing galleries for visitors and are pleased to answer questions and explain how trading works. Exchange gift shops often sell interesting books on investing. Call ahead for free literature and visiting hours.

- New York Stock Exchange
  212-656-3000
  11 Wall Street
  New York, NY 10005

- American Stock Exchange
  212-306-1000
  86 Trinity Place
  New York, NY 10006

- Chicago Board of Trade
  312-435-3500
  141 West Jackson Blvd.
  Chicago, IL 60604

- Chicago Mercantile Exchange
  312-930-1000
  30 South Wacker Drive
  Chicago, IL 60606

- Kansas City Board of Trade
  816-753-7500
  4800 Main Street
  Kansas City, MO 64112

- Boston Stock Exchange
  617-723-9500
  1 Boston Place
  Boston, MA 02108

- Cincinnati Stock Exchange
  513-621-1410
  49 East 4th Street
  Cincinnati, OH 45202

- Pacific Stock Exchange
  415-393-4000
  301 Pine Street
  San Francisco, CA 94104
  or
  233 South Beaudry Avenue
  213-977-4500
  Los Angeles, CA 90012

- Philadelphia Stock Exchange
  215-496-5000
  1900 Market Street
  Philadelphia, PA 19103

- Spokane Stock Exchange
  509-624-4632
  Seafirst Financial Center
  Spokane, WA 99201

In Canada:
- Alberta Stock Exchange
  403-262-7791

- Montreal Stock Exchange
  514-871-2424

- Toronto Stock Exchange
  416-947-4700

- Vancouver Stock Exchange
  604-643-6590

- Winnipeg Stock Exchange
  204-942-8431

How to Find a Company's Headquarters

These reference books are available at most public libraries and brokerage offices:

- *Value Line Investment Survey*
  711 Third Avenue
  New York, NY 10017

- *Standard and Poor's Register*
  Standard and Poor's Corp.
  25 Broadway
  New York, NY 10004

- *Fact Book*
  American Stock Exchange
  Publications Dept.
  86 Trinity Place
  New York, NY 10006

- *NASDAQ Company Directory*
  National Association of
  Securities Dealers
  Book Order Dept.
  9513 Key West Avenue
  Rockville, MD 20850

The Wall Street Zoo

A MENAGERIE OF TERMS

Wow your friends with the latest Wall Street jargon:

- *Beartrap*: A chart pattern, seemingly optimistic, that lures investors into buying a stock before it crashes in price
- *Bears*: Pessimistic investors
- *Bedbugs*: Letters from the SEC to investment bankers asking for corrections or more information before a security can be registered
- *Bulls*: Optimistic investors
- *Cage*: Back room at a brokerage office where cash and securities are handled
- *Cash cow*: Company that predictably earns a lot of cash
- *CATS*: Certificate of Accrual on Treasury Securities, a type of government bond
- *Cats and dogs*: Poor quality stocks; the last to go up in a bull market
- *COLTS*: Continuously offered long-term securities, such as thirty-year bonds

- *Dog and Pony show*: A program or reception during which a new company is presented with great fanfare to potential backers and investors
- *Goldbugs*: Investors who believe gold is the only place to put your money
- *Killer bees*: Lawyers involved in takeovers
- *LYONS*: Liquid Yield Option Notes; a complicated type of bond
- *Nest egg*: Savings account
- *PIGS*: Passive Income Generators; a type of investment, often real estate, that has some tax advantages
- *Red herring*: Preliminary prospectus for a new issue; red ink signals that it's only preliminary
- *Sharks*: Corporate takeover specialists
- *TIGRS*: Treasury Investment Growth Receipts, a type of government bond
- *Turkey*: A dud; a poor investment or a dumb investor

Financial TV Shows

Wall Street Week
PBS
Hosted by Louis Rukeyser, this weekly
show discusses the week's stock market
followed by questions from viewers. A
noted financial expert is questioned by
the program's panel.

Adam Smith's Money World
PBS
Adam Smith is a pen name for a financial
author. His weekly program features
excellent graphic presentations of one
current business topic followed by dis-
cussion with experts.

Nightly Business Report
PBS
A half hour show, Monday through
Friday. Covers topical business news and
the stock market. Excellent coverage of
overseas and domestic financial markets.

Moneyline
PBS
A half-hour show, Monday through
Friday. Covers stock market news and
late-breaking financial stories. Stock tips
and financial insights are valuable to
serious investors.

Wall Street Journal Report
CBS
A half-hour show Sunday mornings. A
team of reporters cover current business
and consumer news. Topics are of
general interest and often include news
about certain industries.

CNN
Cable
Begins coverage of financial news at 6:30
A.M. and provides Wall Street updates on
the half hour each weekday. Has the
largest business news staff in television.

FNN
Cable
Continuous coverage of the financial
markets weekdays from 6 A.M. to 6 P.M.
The ticker tape runs constantly at the
bottom of the TV screen. For those who
want to check a stock's price.

Your Investment Library

Read at least one of these publications on
a regular basis. Clip and save articles that
you don't have time to read right away.
Tackle them on the weekend or on your
vacation.

• *USA Today*: The *"Money"*
section of this daily newspaper gives a
brief synopsis of what's happening on
Wall Street and elsewhere in the investment world. Easy to read.

• *Your local newspaper*: If you live
in a rural area or small-to-medium-sized
town, much of the coverage will be local
and by the wire services. Try to supple-
ment with a national publication.

• *U.S. News & World Report*: This
weekly magazine contains an informative
section on investing and economic news.

• *Money*: A sophisticated monthly
magazine published by Time Warner,Inc.

• *The Wall Street Journal*: Published Monday through Friday. Everything you ever wanted to know about the market, and more.

• *The New York Times*: The Sunday business section gives an excellent overview of the national and global economies, the stock market, and personal investing.

• *Barron's*: A weekly magazine/newspaper by the publisher of *The Wall Street Journal*. Definitive stock tables and coverage of the market. Regular columnists are opinionated and fresh.

Helpful Brochures

The financial section of your Sunday newspaper, or that of *The New York Times*, the daily *Wall Street Journal* and its weekly sister publication, *Barron's*, runs ads from brokerage firms and newsletter publishers offering free brochures and sample publications on investing. Many are well written and informative. If you send away for this free literature, be prepared to receive phone calls from stockbrokers and salespeople.

• *Journey Through a Stock Exchange*
  75 cents
  American Stock Exchange
  Publications Department
  86 Trinity Place
  New York, NY 10006

• *You and the Investment World*
  $3.60
  New York Stock Exchange
  Educational Products
  P.O. Box 4191
  Syosset, NY 11791

• *Guide to Federal Reserve Board Materials*
  free
  Federal Reserve System
  Publications Services
  Washington, DC 20551

• *How the Securities Investor Protection Corporation Protects You*
  free
  SIPC
  805 15th Street NW
  Washington, DC 20005

• *Consumer's Guide to Financial Independence*
  free
  International Association of Financial Planning
  2 Concourse Parkway
  Atlanta, GA 30328

• *Before You Say Yes: 15 Questions to Turn Off an Investment Swindler*
  free
  National Futures Association
  200 West Madison Street
  Chicago, IL 60606

• *Insider's Guide to* The Wall Street Journal
  free
  call the *Journal* at
  212-416-2000

For More Information

Call several of these firms and ask for the name of the director of personnel. Send a letter to that person requesting information on career possibilities. Indicate that while you are still in school and not seeking a specific job now, you wish to prepare for one. *Note:* Many of these corporations have offices in other cities which can be contacted.

- J.C. Bradford & Co.   615-748-9000
  330 Commerce Street
  Nashville, TN 37201

- First Boston Corporation   212-909-2000
  Park Avenue Plaza
  New York, NY 10055

- Goldman, Sachs, and Co.   212-902-1000
  85 Broad Street
  New York, NY 10004

- Hambrecht & Quist Inc.   415-576-3300
  1 Bush Street
  San Francisco, CA 94104

- Shearson Lehman   212-298-2000
    Hutton, Inc.
  American Express Tower C
  World Financial Center
  New York, NY 10285

- Merrill Lynch & Co.   212-637-7455
  World Financial Center
  North Tower
  New York, NY 10281

- Morgan Stanley & Co.   212-703-4000
  1251 Avenue of the Americas
  New York, NY 10020

- PaineWebber, Inc.   212-713-2000
  1285 Avenue of the Americas
  New York, NY 10019

INDEX

ACKNOWLEDGEMENTS AND PHOTO CREDITS

Page 2: © 1988, The Japan National Tourist Organization; p. 8: The Metropolitan Museum of Art, Gift of Ettie Stettheimer, 1953; p. 12: © George Whitley/ Photo Researchers, Inc.; p. 21: AP/ Wide World Photos; p. 22, 42, 78, 95: Culver Pictures Inc.; p. 30, 31, 119 top: New York Stock Exchange Archives; p. 32, 33, 63, 111: New York Public Library Picture Collection; p. 34: Laima Druskis/ Photo Researchers, Inc.; p. 39, 40, 43, 80, 112, 119 bottom: UPI/ Bettman Newsphotos; p. 44, 81: © Leonard Freed/ Magnum Photos; p. 64: The Bettman Archive; p. 71 Robert Phillips/ The Image Bank; p. 77: Don Christiensen; p. 82: Elliot Erwitt/ Magnum Photos; p. 86: Courtesy, Marsh & McLennan Companies, Inc.; p. 96: Robert A. Isaacs/ Photo Researchers, Inc.; p. 106: Ursula Markus/ Photo Researchers, Inc.; p. 114: Museum of the City of New York; p. 117: Philip Jones Griffiths/ Magnum Photos.
Cover art by Donald Christensen
Photo Research: Photosearch Inc.

The author would like to express her appreciation to Marcy Ross and to Norma L. Ginsberg of Blackbirch Graphics for all their help in the preparation of this book.